A WORKBOOK GUIDE TO

BIBLE JOURNALING

SHANNA NOEL & FRIENDS

CONTENTS

TAKE TWO

A Workbook Guide to Bible Journaling
© 2018 DaySpring Cards, Inc. All rights reserved.
Artwork © Shanna Noel. Used by permission.
Second Edition, April 2019

Published by

DaySpring

P.O. Box 1010
Siloam Springs, AR 72761
dayspring.com

Contributing writers: Elaine Davis, Heather Greenwood, Cristin Howell, Jillian Ungerbuehler,
April Crosier, Llanet Fernandez, LaQuisha Hall

Typeset Designer: Suzanne Randolph

Photography by: Jena Stagner from One Beautiful Life Photo

Printed in China.

Prime: 89879
ISBN: 9781684086078

I AM BEYOND EXCITED that you picked up this book and are joining us for some **FUN LESSONS IN BIBLE JOURNALING!**

I HAVE ASKED SOME OF MY SWEET FRIENDS TO SHARE WITH YOU THEIR FAVORITE WAYS TO BIBLE JOURNAL. IN THE FOLLOWING PAGES, YOU WILL FIND INSPIRING ideas full of color, paint, washi tape, fabric, hand-lettering, and more, but I want you to remember that at the heart of

ALL THIS IS JESUS.

In the following pages, we are inviting you to allow your creativity to document your faith story. Another thing I ask that you keep in mind as you flip through these **COLORFUL** pages is that we are sharing some of OUR favorite ways; that doesn't mean that this is the only way. In fact, it is our hope that this would just be a jumping off point for you to find a way that speaks to your heart as you document your faith. Use these tools and steps to set a foundation for your own unique process! We have included some workspace for you to join us right here in this book

& MAKE YOUR MARK!

HAPPY JOURNALING! XOXO
Shanna Noel

SHANNA NOEL

is the founder and owner of Illustrated Faith and the Bible-journaling community, and she stands in awe at what God is doing in their creative community. She lives in Washington State with her husband, Jonathan, and their two daughters, Jaden and Addison. When they aren't covered in paint and Bible journaling, they are working on reclaimed projects around the house or catching up on the latest movie.

WHAT BIBLE JOURNALING MEANS TO SHANNA:

"Bible journaling has been such a freeing experience for me, a chance for me to connect with His beautiful Word in such a meaningful and personal way. I am a visual learner, so the fact that I am able to keep this visual map of my testimony right next to His Word has been a game changer in my life, in my heart, and in my relationship with Jesus."

Shanna's Tip for Beginners:

"My number-one tip for those of you just starting out is to remember what drew you to Bible journaling in the first place. Keep God at the center of your study and build upon that, and everything else will work itself out! Your style will change, your favorite colors or techniques will change, but God never changes! The only thing I regret about Bible journaling is that I didn't start sooner (can you imagine having your whole walk with Jesus documented in this way?), so don't wait until you've mastered all the techniques in this book to start in your Bible. Pick one and run with it!"

ELAINE DAVIS

is a graphic designer for Illustrated Faith and director of the Illustrated Faith Print and Pray Shop. She's an artist, bookworm, and dreamer. She lives in Indiana with her husband, Ian, and kitty, Phoebe. She spends most of her time in Studio Peach, her home-based art studio, which is filled to the brim with a rainbow of paints, buttons, and inspiring bits of paper.

WHAT BIBLE JOURNALING MEANS TO ELAINE:

"I've been an artist since I was old enough to hold a pen or a brush. I've been a Christian longer than that. Finding a way to bring those two huge parts of my life together was truly a game changer. When I'm spending time Bible journaling, I'm growing as a Christian and also growing as an artist. I'm wildly blessed that the Lord leads me to share my heart with others each day through my art. I'm able to connect with so many creatives and I've made countless lasting friendships with our shared interests: creativity and loving Jesus!"

Elaine's Tip for Beginners:

"Inspiration is all around you! I find ideas for my art from all sorts of ordinary avenues. Some of my favorite places to go for inspiration are the children's book section of bookstores, the greeting card aisle, thrift stores, catalogs, and the paint department at the hardware store!"

HEATHER GREENWOOD

is a self-taught mixed media artist residing in the Chicago suburbs with her husband and three kids. She's been Bible journaling for five years and loves experimenting with paint and different techniques and then using what she learns to write tutorials for Illustrated Faith.

WHAT BIBLE JOURNALING MEANS TO HEATHER:

"Bible journaling has changed my life. I am able to have a relationship with God that I struggled to have before. I've been a believer since I was a kid, but I never felt a love for the Word of God like I do now. Being able to study the Word in my creative heart language has shown me how to have that relationship with God that I always craved and the way He created me for."

Heather's Tip for Beginners:

"My biggest tip is to let go of perfection and enjoy the worship. Experiment, try new techniques, and just have fun spending sweet time in the Word."

CRISTIN HOWELL

lives in Southern Oregon with her husband, John, and their four little dogs. She loves to spend time in her crafty space, sewing and creating. When she's not doing those things, you can find her at a vintage fair or on a hike at a nearby trail. From the very moment she saw Bible journaling on Instagram, she fell in love and knew she HAD to try it as soon as possible.

WHAT BIBLE JOURNALING MEANS TO CRISTIN:

"Bible journaling has transformed my spiritual life! I used to feel like such a Bible-reading failure! Why couldn't I stick with it? When I started journaling, I felt like I had a new language to worship Jesus! My heart has been transformed and I look forward to spending time with the Lord in His Word. He teaches me new things and I love being able to document my spiritual growth in this way."

Cristin's Tip for Beginners:

"Just keep going, no matter what! Even if you drop an inkpad face down on your page, squish paint all over your pretty bows, or stick your alphas on backwards–it will be okay. I've done all these things! Don't let anything (or anyone!) steal your joy for journaling."

JILLIAN UNGERBUEHLER

is a thirtysomething Florida native, currently outnumbered by her husband and two sons. (There is only one pink thing in her house!) She began Bible journaling in early 2016 and instantly became hooked! When she's not putting stickers in the margins of her Bible, she is most likely cooking, or napping.

WHAT BIBLE JOURNALING MEANS TO JILLIAN:

"Bible journaling is a sweet reminder that God is good to me. I had a creative hobby that I loved, but if I was being honest, it had taken its place in my heart before God. As I turned away from that hobby I learned about Bible journaling. Bible journaling became a way for me to still use my hands to create beautiful things, but this time God (and His Word) were at the center of my creative time. How amazing and kind is He?!"

Jillian's Tip for Beginners:

"Nervous about 'messing up' your Bible? I get it! Before trying a new technique in the margin, why not take a test drive on a scrap piece of paper or in a notebook? It's a quick and easy way to get rid of those jitters. Then, just go for it!"

APRIL CROSIER

is from the Atlanta area and is a firm believer in big praise hands, Sunday naps, and coffee at night. She's married to the world's most hunkiest fella, and together they have four children through God's miraculous grace and the beauty of adoption. She is passionate about shining light on the imperfections of life and testifying to the glory received by God when we talk about our own hard seasons with others. When she's not painting in her Bible, you can find her growing all sorts of garden goodness, baking delicious treats, and tending to her small flock of backyard chickens.

WHAT BIBLE JOURNALING MEANS TO APRIL:

"Bible journaling for me is a beautiful collision of worship—it's taking the passion for creativity that God purposely placed in my heart and pairing it with His Word for us. Each page, each margin, is an expression of love, grace, beauty, and desire to become more aligned with my heavenly Father."

April's Tip for Beginners:

"JUMP IN, FRIEND! There's no right or wrong way to enter into the presence of God—and you truly can NOT mess anything up. Throw some paint haphazardly in your margin right this very second, take a deep breath, and get ready for an incredible adventure unlike any other!"

LLANET FERNANDEZ

Hello, my name is Llanet (pronounced Janet), and many of you know me by my social media name: @topknotsandjesus. I live in sunny Miami, Florida, with my husband and my two Australian shepherds. Being part of the Illustrated Faith Creative Team has allowed me to meet people from all over the world and inspire them creatively and spiritually. I am a true Bible nerd, I love all things Jesus, coffee is my fuel, and tacos are life. I have been Bible journaling for only a year and half, and it has completely changed me creatively. When I'm not Bible journaling or creating, I love photography, interior design, writing, and spending quality time with my family.

WHAT BIBLE JOURNALING MEANS TO LLANET:

"Bible journaling is a way to embellish an already beautiful love letter from God. When I Bible journal, I feel like I'm submerging myself deep in His Word. His Word is alive and evokes peace. As I ponder His Word, I allow it to inspire creativity. The best part of journaling is spending time with God and allowing His truth to take root in my heart. I call my Bible journaling sessions 'little dates with God.'"

Llanet's Tip for Beginners:

"BE YOU! It's that simple. Never look at or compare yourself to someone else; your talent, your gift was YOUniquely designed for you. God created you different from anyone else in the world; you were meant to stand out, so when others see your pages, let it be a direct reflection of what God brings out of you.

LAQUISHA HALL

is from Baltimore, Maryland. She loves all things creative and has been an artist since childhood. She is especially a fan of Bible journaling, planning, happy mail, and hand lettering (all of which she has done for the past three years). Through her social media (@confidentcanvas) she creates and shares her own work as well as hosts workshops to fuel the creative abilities of those she inspires.

WHAT BIBLE JOURNALING MEANS TO LAQUISHA:

"Bible journaling is taking on one of the awesome characteristics of my heavenly Father: Creator. God so beautifully created the world in six days; He allows me the space and place to create in my Bible. I get the divine opportunity to be able to worship and draw closer to Him by reading, studying, and illustrating His Word. Essentially, I have craft time with God. He took time to craft me—I owe Him this time back."

LaQuisha's Tip for Beginners:

"Begin with your level of comfortability. It is inspiring to see photos, blogs, and social media accounts filled with beautifully decorated Bible pages. However, do not compare your work in whatever form and at whatever level you create it. Remember, Bible journaling is not a competition or a race to first place; it is precious time with our God who desires to spend time with us."

What is: BIBLE JOURNALING?

This is a wonderful question, thank you so much for asking!

YOU SEE, UPON FIRST GLANCE IT MAY APPEAR TO BE ONE THING:

a hobby, a way to "decorate" your Bible, something bright and shiny, or even just the latest "trend." Bible journaling for me is so much more than that. Bible journaling is a way to document, remember, and celebrate what God is doing through my life and in my heart in a creative way. I don't know about you, but I have always been a visual learner; show me black and white text and I may take away 50 percent of it (if I am lucky), but pair that with a photo or a visual way of telling the story and you have me!

Please don't get me wrong, the Bible is a story about JESUS, not about me, but by documenting what I am learning through His Word and through a relationship with Him, I am then able to use that as a resource on my journey and to share that testimony with those around me.

IN THIS BOOK

WE ARE GOING TO TEACH YOU THE TECHNIQUES BEHIND BIBLE JOURNALING

but I want you to promise me right here and right now that you will remember the true heart behind it and use this book as a tool to tell those HUGE GOD stories in your life!

HERE IS THE TRUTH, FRIEND (are you ready for it?)

there is no RIGHT or WRONG way to Bible journal.

I know what you are thinking: Why are you telling me this? I thought you were going to teach me ALL THE THINGS!

We will teach you the techniques that we use to Bible journal, we will teach you our favorite ways to add a little paint to your pages or how to rock a sticker, but what I want YOU to do is to take those techniques and put your own twist on them. Since Bible journaling has taken off on Pinterest and Instagram I have had people come into class and say,

"I HAVE COPIED ALL OF YOUR ENTRIES AND I AM JUST NOT GETTING ANYTHING OUT OF IT!"

Well, friend, that is because you have documented MY testimony in YOUR Bible.

Now is the time to document YOUR GOD STORIES! TELL THEM, PAINT THEM, SHARE THEM! SHOUT THEM FROM THE ROOFTOPS! This is the time to set aside all expectations about what your Bible is going to look like, hand it over to God, and just allow yourself to rest in this time of worship!

Where DO I Start?

Once people get on board with the idea of Bible journaling, usually one of the first questions that I get is "Where do I start? Page 1, Genesis 1:1?" The truth is that unlike a regular book or art journal, we don't always start on page 1 in our Bibles; instead we are taken to where God leads us, or to where our pastor spoke from last Sunday, or to a verse we were reminded of in conversation with a friend.

THAT IS WHERE I WANT YOU TO START.

SOME OF MY FAVORITE WAYS TO SPARK A BIBLE JOURNALING SESSION:

Sermon notes, prayer, daily Bible reading, a worship song, devotional, a verse a friend reminded you of, and even random inspiration (we will talk more about this later!)

WHAT NOW?
You open up your Bible, read the verse, AND START CREATING?

I know most of us want to jump right into the creative part, but remember you are documenting what God is laying on YOUR HEART through the message of His Word, and sometimes that takes some time. I want you to pray about it and allow it to sink into your heart; don't just take things at face value.

Once you have prayed about it and have a message on your heart that you want to document, **NOW** IS WHEN WE GET TO CREATE!

Now, remember earlier when we talked about NOT having rules? I know that idea won't work for all of you so I am going to share a couple things I try to do when I am Bible journaling. In general, I almost always have a LARGE TITLE, something that I can look at right away and remember exactly WHY I am documenting this in my Bible. Then I will pair that with a visual way to tell that story, an icon of some sort, followed by some journaling. I almost always finish off a page with a *date* (I LOVE having the dates in my Bible; it really shows you the journey He takes you on!) and a TAB at the top of the page. Now friend, because I know YOU are most likely a visual learner as well, we have prepared this book with lots of pictures, tips, and tricks to take you through that process time and time again. Take this book at your own pace, don't feel the need to complete a page your first time, and allow yourself the space and grace to make this journey your own!

WHAT SHOULD I JOURNAL IN? GREAT QUESTION!

You will see a lot of us using journaling Bibles, but please feel free to take these same techniques and apply them to your journal, traveler's notebook, planner, art journal, scrapbook, pocket pages, etc.

THE POSSIBILITIES ARE ENDLESS!

don't worry, friend,
WE WILL DO THIS TOGETHER!   XOXO
Shanna Noel

GO FOR IT

TAKE ONE

SECTION 1

SECTION 1:1

ALL PEOPLE, ALL NATIONS

For this entry I am working in

EPHESIANS 3.

There's been so much great conversation on unity and diversity in the Bible journaling community, something I am so thankful for! Through this entry I am praying that I continue to be surrounded by those powerful conversations and that God is always at the center of them!

SHANNA NOEL

BLANK PAGE

One of the scariest things most Bible journalers face
(well, most artists for that matter) is

the fear of the blank page.

The fear of "ruining your Bible." Friends, I TOTALLY GET THAT!

Do you want to know my favorite way to jump
over that fear wall you have built for yourself?

PAINT! YES! GLORIOUS, COLORFUL, SUPER MESSY, BUT ALL KINDS OF FUN...PAINT!

NOW KEEP IN MIND

that we aren't going for perfection here.
We are just breaking the white page syndrome
and building ourselves a beautiful background to build upon.

TECHNIQUE · TECHNIQUE

One of my favorite ways to add paint to a page is with the scraping method. Grab some acrylic paint an old gift card, and you have just about everything you will need to add some beautiful paint marks to your page. When I am getting ready to paint a page I do a little prep work, adding a Bible mat under my page and bring some baby wipes

(FRIENDS, I AM MESSY!)

and then I am set!

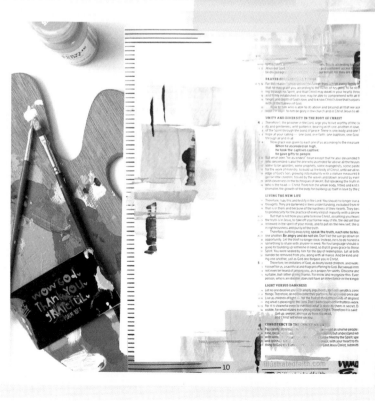

- Apply a small amount of paint to the edge of your gift card or paint card, keeping in mind the more you apply and the wider you apply, the wider your mark will be.

- Bring the card to the page, apply tension, and drag down the page where you want the paint! Pull the card up, and you've got yourself one beautiful paint mark on your page!

- Repeat these steps until you have the desired effect you are looking for!

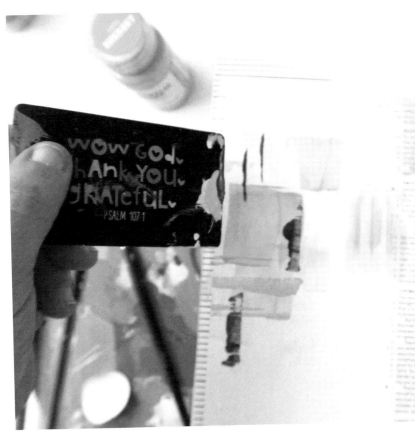

A COUPLE OF THINGS TO KEEP IN MIND.

This takes a little practice getting used to so don't be afraid to practice on a piece of scrap paper until you've got the hang of it. Also, be mindful of the colors you pick. You want colors to go together and have a balance to them.

I typically will pull out the supplies I know I will want to add later to my color palette, and then play around with how much of each color I want to add with paint. As you can see from my page, I added a fair amount of the lighter colors (in groups that make a visual triangle across my page) and then added less of the darker colors on top. This is just my personal style for this page; the more you play with it, the more you will find your style as well. Because we are adding such thin layers of paint (and depending on the quality of paint you use) these layers are going to dry super-fast, allowing you to work on your next step!

• **Acrylic Paint**
• **Paint Card**
• **Baby Wipes**
• **Paint brushes**
• **illustrating Bible:**
   DaySpring & Illustrated Faith
• **Illustrated Faith Bible Mat**

When you are working on your titles and journaling, I think one thing to keep in mind is

WHAT ARE YOU TAKING AWAY FROM THIS PASSAGE?

What do you want to remember next time you flip to those pages and what are the words you want to mark in your testimony? There are lots of ways to get this point across, but today I wanted to use this beautiful journaling card from the All People, All Nations line from Illustrated Faith.

Journaling cards are great for so many reasons. You can make a little hidden journal with them by applying washi tape at the top and using it as a little flip-up.

You can also run them through your printer or typewriter if you want to use something other than your handwriting.

TECHNIQUE · TECHNIQUE

TECHNIQUE · TECHNIQUE

Some journaling prompts to help get you started:
Thank You, Father, for...
   These words speak to my heart...
   Hear my voice...
   I am thankful that...

THE VERY FIRST THING I DID

I pulled out my alphabet stamps and stamped AMEN at the top.

A lot of my journaling is done through prayer, so that word seems to be literally stamped all over my Bible!

I added a little washi tape to stick my journaling card on the page and this part is done!

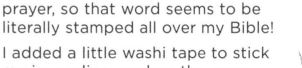
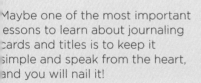

Maybe one of the most important lessons to learn about journaling cards and titles is to keep it simple and speak from the heart, and you will nail it!

TECHNIQUE · TECHNIQUE

SUPPLIES · SUPPLIES

- Illustrated Faith Bible Mat
- Illustrated Faith Journaling Pen
- Amy Tangerine Alphabet Stamps
- Illustrated Faith Journaling Card
  All People All Nations
- Illustrated Faith Criss Cross Washi Tape
  (Black and White)
- Illustrating Bible from DaySpring and Illustrated Faith

Finishing touches are what really bring a page together, and they are one of my FAVORITE PARTS!

You have already done the hard work of starting at that blank page, pouring your heart out through journaling,

now we just get to add some beautiful finishing touches!

One of my favorite ways to add those finishing touches is with art marks. Now this is just a term I use for those fun little doodles I add at the end of my process. For this page, I wanted to show you my go-to method: **art marks with Neocolor II crayons!** Neocolor crayons are water-soluble artist crayons made from high-quality, lightfast pigments. When you use these, you will notice that they are softer than a colored pencil but denser than a wax crayon. I like to use them on their own, but you can also use them to create a beautiful watercolor effect.

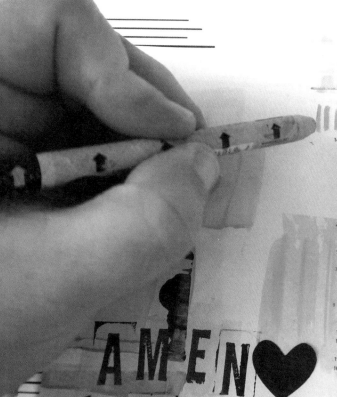

874

11 to the rulers and authorities in the heavens. This is according to his eternal purpose accomplished in Christ
12 13 Jesus our Lord. In him we have holdness and confident access through faith in him. So then I ask you not to
be discouraged over my afflictions on your behalf, for they are your glory.

PRAYER FOR SPIRITUAL POWER

14 15 16 For this reason I kneel before the Father from whom every family in heaven and on earth is named. I pray
that he may grant you, according to the riches of his glory, to be strengthened with power in your inner be-
17 ing through his Spirit, and that Christ may dwell in your hearts through faith. I pray that you, being rooted
18 and firmly established in love, may be able to comprehend with all the saints what is the length and width,
19 height and depth of God's love, and to know Christ's love that surpasses knowledge, so that you may be filled
with all the fullness of God.
20 Now to him who is able to do above and beyond all that we ask or think according to the power that
21 works in us— to him be glory in the church and in Christ Jesus to all generations, forever and ever. Amen.

UNITY AND DIVERSITY IN THE BODY OF CHRIST

4 2 Therefore I, the prisoner in the Lord, urge you to live worthy of the calling you have received, with all humil-
3 ity and gentleness, with patience, bearing with one another in love, making every effort to keep the unity
4 of the Spirit through the bond of peace. There is one body and one Spirit—just as you were called to one
5 6 hope at your calling— one Lord, one faith, one baptism, one God and Father of all, who is above all and
through all and in all.
7 8 Now grace was given to each one of us according to the measure of Christ's gift. For it says:

When he ascended on high,
he took the captives captive;
he gave gifts to people.

9 10 But what does "he ascended" mean except that he also descended to the lower parts of the earth? The one
11 who descended is also the one who ascended far above all the heavens, to fill all things. And he himself gave
12 some to be apostles, some prophets, some evangelists, some pastors and teachers, equipping the saints
13 for the work of ministry, to build up the body of Christ, until we all reach unity in the faith and in the knowl-
14 edge of God's Son, growing into maturity with a stature measured by Christ's fullness. Then we will no longer be little children, tossed by the waves and blown around by every wind of teaching, by human cunning
15 with cleverness in the techniques of deceit. But speaking the truth in love, let us grow in every way into him
16 who is the head—Christ. From him the whole body, fitted and knit together by every supporting ligament,
promotes the growth of the body for building up itself in love by the proper working of each individual part.

LIVING THE NEW LIFE

17 Therefore, I say this a...stify in the Lord: You should no longer
18 thoughts. They are...

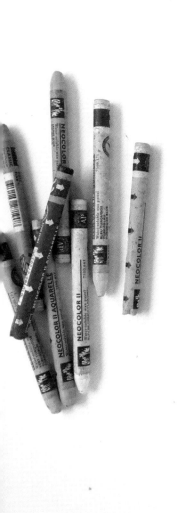

When applying art marks to this page I am going to follow the pattern I already set with the paint (see pages 22-23) and use similar or tone-on-tone colors to add depth to the layers. I love playing with different art marks like crosses, hashmarks, tiny hearts, polka dots, lines, smudges, and little scribbles, and combining them all or any combination of them to make a fun and playful pattern! Again, this is something you can practice on a scratch piece of paper until you find some art marks that you love and then bring them into your Bible.

Pay attention to creating thoughtful clusters that follow the patterns you have already set on your page, or be brave and just break all the rules!

Once again, make them your own and HAVE FUN WITH IT!

- Caran d'ache Neocolor II Artists' Crayons
- Illustrated Faith Bible Mat
- Illustrating Bible from DaySpring and Illustrated Faith

SUPPLIES · SUPPLIES

WHAT I LEARNED FROM SHANNA NOEL:

best tips | what I took away | things to try next time

date _____

SECTION 1:2

HE GOES BEFORE US

ELAINE DAVIS

PSALM 66:12 ESV

Lately my husband, Ian, and I have been navigating through some uncharted territory as we make plans to start our family. We're about to begin fertility treatments and so much of it is scary! We often have no idea what's going on or what the next steps are, so we feel like we're shuffling through it blindly. But God! He goes before us.

I came across **PSALM 66:12 ESV** and it hit me over the head with a blank map.

A map that only the Lord can read,
but we must use it to stay on course strictly through trust.

The passage reads:

"YOU LET MEN RIDE OVER OUR HEADS;
WE WENT THROUGH FIRE AND THROUGH WATER; YET YOU HAVE
BROUGHT US OUT TO A PLACE OF ABUNDANCE."

He leads so many scared, lost souls through treacherous terrain and adversity to a place of abundance and miracles. We trust that the Scriptures are true and lean into His provision of direction.

THE VERY FIRST THING I DID

was choose the main focus piece
I would use on this page.

I usually like my artwork to have a *"star"*
of the show, or some sort of anchor that catches your eye,
then a design to give the composition some movement.

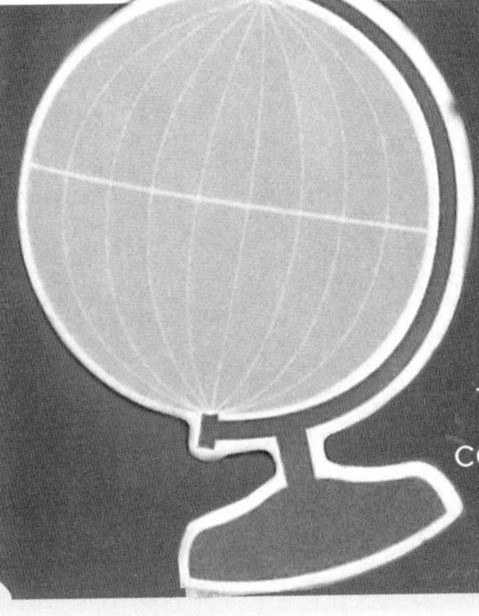

"star" My focus piece is
this chipboard globe,
which seemed very fitting
for prayers of direction.

The image in my head was a pattern radiating out from a central point like a sunbeam to represent starting a journey and spreading outward to follow God's plan.

I placed my chipboard globe around center height, near the crease of my Bible, to create my vertex (central point).

Then I used a stencil and a pencil to lightly trace two lines radiating from where the globe will be.

NOW FOR THE PATTERN

To create an overall design right on a Bible page, my go-to tool is a stencil. I have a huge stash of them and they're a great investment because you can use them over and over again! This triangle pattern stencil has a brilliant geometric design that really packs a big punch!

Yay!

LET'S MOVE ON TO STENCILING!

Creating a crisp edge with a stencil is super easy—all you have to do is create a mask.

A mask simply means using a barrier to cover certain areas of your page in order to stop your medium from going through your stencil.

In this case, I used a sheet of common copy paper that I cut in half vertically. I aligned the edges of my copy paper pieces with the pencil lines I drew, then carefully aligned it with the edges of my stencil. It would be pretty tricky to hold all three components in place as I applied my color, so I used washi tape to secure them and temporarily attach them to my page.

With my mask and stencil in place, I used a blender tool to apply ink through the stencil. You can do this with all sorts of items:

BLENDER TOOL
BLENDING STUMP
SPONGES
DAUBERS
A PAPER TOWEL
EVEN A BABY WIPE

The blender tool I used has interchangeable pads so you can use it for different colors.

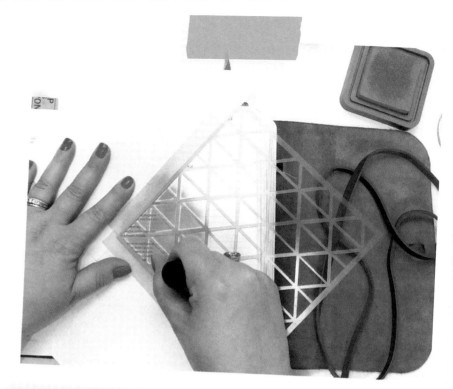

To apply the color, pat your blender onto the ink pad, then scrub it over the stencil gently in small circles like you're brushing your teeth. Then remove your stencil and mask to reveal your design!

SUPPLIES

- **Copy Paper**
- **Pencil**
- **Washi Tape**
- **Tim Holtz Blending Tool**
- **Heidi Swapp Geometric Stencil**
- **Tim Holtz Distress Oxide Ink Pad:**
    Picked Raspberry
- **Bella Blvd Pop Quiz Ciao Chip Icons**
- **Journaling Bible**
    Crossway ESV Single Column Leather Wrap

There are so many different styles of Bible journaling,
but the style you'll see me use 99 percent of the time is

A LAYERED, SCRAPPY VIBE.

I've been scrapbooking for 19 years, so much of my paper crafting
has been done like this. It's absolutely my style, alongside some
stitching, doodling, and mixed media.
That being said, typically what I do next when creating a Bible page is
choose the bigger layering elements.

I'm being completely honest when I say

OFTEN MY SUPPLIES AND PALETTE CHOICES COME FROM TWO PLACES.

1. The color palette or collection of the focus piece I choose.

2. Whatever I find lying around my workspace.

You wouldn't believe the bits and treasures I find hiding in little dishes on my desk. In this case, several of the paper scraps I layered behind the globe were hanging out in my workspace, so I grabbed them. Journaling with your leftover scraps often results in unique and interesting shapes.

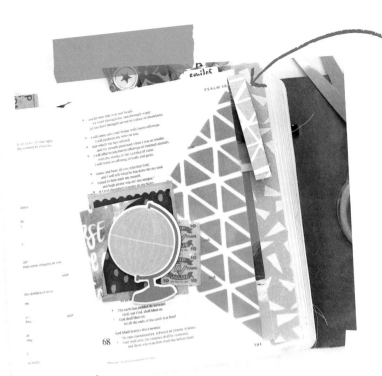

After layering up some papers and ephemera pieces behind the globe, I added some longer scraps on the edge of the page to balance some of the colors. It would have looked perfectly fine without them, but I like a lot of detail. Once I have all the pieces layered how I want them, I often take a photo of the layers just in case I don't get them back exactly the way they were after moving them.

For this page, I thought the layers could benefit from some black inking on the edges. It's so easy and really makes the lighter colored pieces pop! You can see me taking each piece and simply rubbing the edge on the ink pad to outline it. You can also do this with a blender tool or sponge.

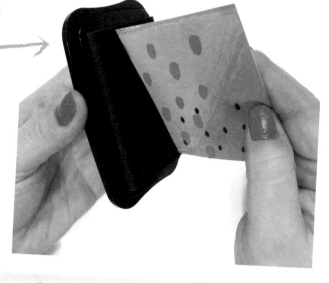

Then, I re-stacked the pieces and carefully put a bit of adhesive on the back of each one using a tape runner to hold them in place. I don't adhere the bottom layer to the page yet to give myself the freedom to move the entire cluster.

Before adhering the chipboard piece, I used my sewing machine to do some messy stitching around the cluster and did the same with the scraps on the edge of the page. I also wadded up some messy thread scraps behind the globe for some texture, **which is SO FUN,** don't you think!?

After gluing down the clusters, the main portion of the page is done.

SUPPLIES
SUPPLIES

- Vintage Tickets
- Solid Washi Tape
- Sew-ology Thread Spools
- Bella Blvd Pop Stickers:
     Quiz Sticky Mix Cardstock
- Staz-On Ink Pad: Jet Black
- Scallop Edge Scissors
- Scotch Quick-Dry Tacky Glue
- Glue Dots
- Tombow Mono Dots Adhesive
- Illustrated Faith 12x12 Paper Pack:
    All People, All Nations
- Bella Blvd Pop Quiz Patterned Paper: Goofing Off

Guys. This is my FAVORITE part of any page!

I LIVE FOR DETAILS.

The finishing touches really put my mark on my art.
If you were to take a peek into my supply stash, you'd see
an entire dresser full of embellishments and alpha stickers.

**THEY'RE LIKE THE SPRINKLES ON TOP
OF A DELICIOUS STRAWBERRY ICE CREAM CONE!**

YUM!

To continue the list of my favorite supplies of all time
(YOU MIGHT WANT TO GRAB A SODA—THIS COULD TAKE AWHILE!)...

I want to add stamps. When you purchase a stamp set, you're getting an incredible bang for your buck. If you care for them correctly, you can get thousands of uses out of stamp sets. I love using them for backgrounds, titles, and creating repeating patterns, but on this page, I also used an accent stamp to create visual interest on my Bible page. The asterisk shape of the stamp also echoes the pattern of the blue arrow on the globe.

After stamping, I couldn't resist adding some **SPRINKLES** to my globe! I added a tiny wood veneer geo location symbol to represent where God might take us in our fertility journey and added an arrow sticker that I stamped with the word "tRuST." When I'm adding other embellishments to my creations, I usually shop my stash by color palette. I pull little bits and bobs that work with the colors in my focus piece, paint, or patterned paper.

Once I add my title, I focus on my journaling, which is arguably the most important aspect of your Bible pages.

WHY ARE WE CREATING IN OUR BIBLES IN THE FIRST PLACE?

Because we want to strengthen our relationship with the Lord and work through our faith journey. Our journaling allows us to put to paper what our hearts are telling us. Writing out our prayers connects us to Scripture in a very real way and puts a sort of "heart stamp" on what we're working through when we read it. For this entry my journaling reflected how I was feeling about being in a season of waiting.

Acknowledging our weaknesses allows God to breathe strength and guidance into our lives. If you don't do anything else on a Bible journaling page, do this:

PULL OUT A FAVORITE PEN & GET TO WORK POURING YOUR HEART OUT TO THE LORD!

- **Illustrated Faith Pen**
- **Recollections Enamel Dots**
- **Studio Calico Wood Veneer Shapes**
- **Studio G Wood Block Alpha Stamps**
- **Illustrated Faith Date It Rotary Stamp**
- **Illustrated Faith Say It Loud Sticker Sheet: All People, All Nations**

- **Illustrated Faith Highlighter Washi Tape**
- **Bella Blvd Puffy Star Stickers: Punch Mix**
- **Illustrated Faith Stamp Set: Fruit of the Spirit**
- **American Crafts Thickers: Other Half**
- **Glossy Accents Dimensional Medium by Ranger**

best tips | what I took away | things to try next time

date _____

SECTION 1:3

SPIRIT LEAD ME

PSALM 143:10 ESV

"Teach me to do your will, for you are my God! Let your good Spirit lead me on level ground!" One of the things I love to do is go through ephemera pieces and just pick one. On the back is a Scripture reference. I sit and meditate on the verse and then pray about it. I loved the "Spirit lead me" ephemera piece and instantly knew I wanted this verse to be a prayer for guidance and to be led to do His will rather than my own.

We are going to start with one of my favorite techniques, which is to scrape paint using a paint card.

TECHNIQUE · TECHNIQUE

The beauty of the paint card is you can do small strokes or large and bold paint strokes. It is like a paint brush but helps you get a thinner coverage. "Scraping paint on" allows for the paint to go on very thinly, which makes it transparent. This also means the paint dries quickly so you can layer new colors on top without them mixing and getting muddy.

I like to start with the lighter colors first and then add on darker colors over the top.

THE VERY FIRST THING I DID

was choose the paint colors. I pick colors that coordinate with the ephemera piece I chose earlier to meditate on. I usually stick to two or three colors, plus white.

Second step is to dip the edge of your paint card into your lightest color and then scrape the edge along your Bible page.

If you are using a tube paint, you will squeeze a tiny bit on the edge of the card instead of dipping it in the paint. Now, this is where you just have fun letting whatever happens happen, whether it's small strokes or large strokes. You have to let go of control because the strokes are not as controlled as a paint brush. I like to have three or five *(odd numbers are appealing from a design standpoint)* paint sections, leaving room for your title and journaling.

Once you are done with one color, repeat with another color.

HAVE FUN LAYERING THE COLORS.

Unless I'm doing a rainbow page, I usually stick to only two to three colors for the base layer. We will be adding more color later, so you want to start with just a few. If I feel like I used too much color or it's too dark, I will use the same technique with white acrylic paint on top of it to tone it down a bit. For this reason, you want to have white on hand.

- **ESV Journaling Bible**
- **Illustrated Faith Bible Mat**
- **Illustrated Faith Paint Cards**
- **Assorted Acrylic Craft Paints**
- **Illustrated Faith Acrylic Paint Set**

SUPPLIES · SUPPLIES

At this point you will feel like your page is kind of plain and needs something. This is where you're going to build onto your foundation. I like to use fun mark making stamps to add more color and to really add to those painted sections. This is where I start to look at some of the other stickers and ephemera I want to add to the page to see if there are more colors I want on my background to tie it all together. What makes mixed media "MIXED MEDIA" is using two or more different mediums. We've used acrylic paint for the base and now we will use ink. You want to stick to pigment or chalk inks for stamp pads, or Faber-Castell Big Brush Pitt Pens for stamping. These inks usually do not bleed through your Bible pages. Again, pick colors that coordinate with any ephemera pieces you plan on adding to your page.

Pick a stamp you like and attach it to an acrylic block. I like to add the stamp to the edge of the block to make it easier to stamp all over the page and easier to get on edges and the middle of the binding .

1.

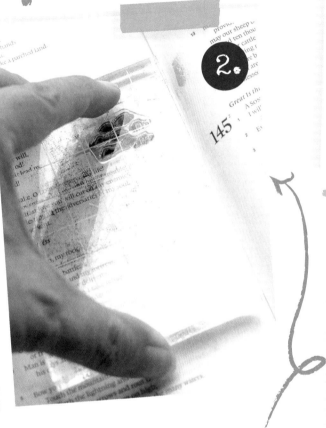

2.

Add ink to your stamp. If you are using the Big Brushes, you'll swipe the color over the stamp. If you are using a stamp pad, you'll tap lightly on the stamp pad to fill your stamp with color.

3.

You will "kiss" the page with your stamp.

SUPPLIES SUPPLIES

- **Illustrated Faith Stamp Set:**
  All People All Nations
- **Illustrated Faith Element Stamp Set**
- **Faber-Castell Big Brush Pitt Pens**

TECHNIQUE · TECHNIQUE

You don't want to stamp too light or too hard. Think of it like you are kissing someone's cheek. If this is your first time stamping, I recommend practicing on a sheet of paper until you are comfortable. That being said, don't expect perfection when you are stamping in your Bible either. Let go of control and enjoy the process. On this page, I wanted to add some orange so I grabbed another stamp set to add more stamping.

FINISHING TOUCHES:
Layering Ephemera, Stickers, Journaling, and a Date

This is where we are going to **CONTINUE BUILDING LAYERS** on top of our background.

First, let's highlight the verse(s) we are focused on. I used a Faber-Castell Big Brush Marker again to swipe color over the verse.

Second, let's add our title. Since the ephemera piece is my title, I'm going to use that, and it places nicely next to the verse.

Third, I am going to build on more layers by finding coordinating ephemera, tabs, and stickers and start placing them around my page, *keeping in mind the painted sections*.

I like having this flower stick out from under the title as it brings all the colors together. I used a tape runner to adhere the paper pieces. For the big flower I only put tape on the left side so that I can lift up the flower to see the Scripture behind it if needed.

Once we're happy with where everything is placed, we add some journaling and a date stamp.

- **StazOn Ink Pad**
- **Illustrated Faith Washi Tape**
- **Illustrated Faith Pen Set**
- **Illustrated Faith Date-It Stamp**
- **Illustrated Faith Words Sticker Booklet**
- **Illustrated Faith Ephemera Pack and Cardstock Stickers:**
  All People All Nations

TECHNIQUE · TECHNIQUE

I also wanted to add more yellow to the page since there is a big yellow spot in the flower. I grabbed some yellow washi tape and tore it in pieces and put the pieces around my page. I stuck to odd numbers and kept in mind the little art sections I had created on the background when placing it. I tore little hexagon stickers from the border sticker in the coordinating cardstock sticker sheet. If you don't like the torn look, use scissors.

best tips | what I took away | things to try next time

date _____

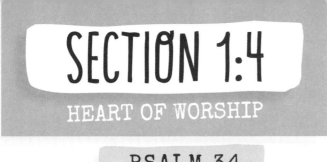

CRISTIN HOWELL

PSALM 34

I love journaling in the Psalms because it's a great place to offer a heart of worship to the Lord. The more I learn about the Lord, the more I experience His goodness. Draw near, friends, His goodness awaits!

TECHNIQUE · TECHNIQUE

Before I start attaching stickers and printables, I like to map out the page visually: Where will I journal and place my elements? How do I want to focus on the Scripture that I'm using? Highlighting the passage also keeps me from accidentally covering it with paint or other embellishments, or even journaling the wrong page.

THE VERY FIRST THING I DID

I highlighted this portion of the Psalm using a printable sticker from Scripture Overlays set in the Illustrated Faith Print and Pray Shop. Printing a digital set onto clear sticker paper (or a clear transparency sheet) creates a see-through sticker that will show the Scripture underneath. This "Amen!" text sticker is one of many options available in the digital shop. But think outside specific highlighting products, because any sticker can highlight a verse section.

TECHNIQUE · TECHNIQUE

Clear stickers also add zero bulk to your page since they are perfectly flat! You can print your own stickers at home by selecting sticker paper that works with your printer (inkjet, laser), or you can have a print shop do this for you by bringing the specialty paper to them.

I printed this sticker at home and trimmed the sticker just around the edges. Since it is clear, it's not necessary to cut it out perfectly.

ANOTHER GREAT POINT:

if you don't enjoy cutting out digital elements, you may love creating with clear stickers.

At this time I swipe acrylic paint onto the page as a base. I like to see the paint color peek around the elements (which I will put on the page later). If I use a color on a page, I try to repeat that color at least three times to achieve a good visual balance.

Here, I used a light pink acrylic paint and applied it from the edge of the words to the edge of the page. I used a Bible mat under the page to protect the pages underneath from accidental paint splotches. Acrylic paint does not bleed through the page, and it should dry quickly if using a thin coat.

SUPPLIES

- **Illustrated Faith Bible Mat**
- **Clear Sticker Paper: Avery 8665**
- **Illustrated Faith Print and Pray Shop:** Scripture Overlays Digital Set
- **Acrylic Paint: Apple Barrel Paint 21464E Cameo Pink**

WHAT COMES NEXT?
Layering Paper

Next, I built the main part of the page while keeping an eye on the journaling section. The very process of journaling I find to be meditative. As I dwell on Scripture, I start thinking about what I will write on the page, whether it will be a prayer or specifically what I'm learning. Sometimes it takes a while for the right words to form, and sometimes the words arrive before I begin.

Here, I sliced up a piece of patterned paper from the Illustrated Faith Fruit of the Spirit collection to build a bit of texture into the background. I trimmed two strips of paper approximately 1.25" x 5" and added a 3" x 4" card from the same collection. The card was a part of the patterned paper, so I simply cut it out. *Don't forget the B side of your patterned papers! I love to check the reverse side for more options and patterns.*

I arranged the strips into an upside-down *L* shape with the card on top, trimming the strips as necessary. I added the apple ephemera pieces and adhered them first onto the card and pulled the strips of paper around the main piece so that they accent the fruit but don't overpower the focal point. I find that arranging paper pieces is most satisfying when there are a few pieces to group together in a cluster. The patterns and texture bring the eye to a focused point on the page. Using patterned paper is another way to fill out an area of the page where you want a little extra something.

After shuffling the pieces around a bit, I lifted the edge of the pieces and used a tape runner to add adhesive to the page without removing all the pieces. Using a tape runner (dry adhesive) to adhere the elements to the Bible page prevents the thin pages from wrinkling.

I like to mix different alpha stickers together, not just because it looks fun, but it's a great way to stretch an alpha sheet that's missing a few key letters. I arranged my stickers on the edge of a clear ruler and moved it around until I found the right sticker placement.

TECHNIQUE TECHNIQUE

SUPPLIES SUPPLIES

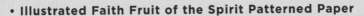

- **Illustrated Faith Fruit of the Spirit Patterned Paper**
- **Illustrated Faith Fruit of the Spirit Ephemera Die Cuts**
- **Bella Blvd Wonky Alphas: Oreo Black**
- **Illustrated Faith Homespun Alpha: Black-eyed Pea**
- **Black and White Small Striped Washi: American Crafts**

LET'S TALK FABRIC BOW CLIPS!

This is one of my all-time favorite ways to top a page.
I love bows—because when my Bible is closed,
all my tabs and bows are still on display.

THERE'S JUST SOMETHING IRRESISTIBLE ABOUT THAT!

To make a cute fabric bow, cut two 1.5" x 7" strips of coordinating fabric or one 1.5" x 14" strip folded in half. Then, adhere the strips (printed sides facing out) using a small amount of liquid glue.

Side Tip: Use a paintbrush to apply the glue if you're making a bunch of bows, and be sure to take the glue to the edges of the fabric to prevent fraying. Also, I like to use a mini hair straightener to "iron" my fabric perfectly flat.

1.

Next, thread the fabric through the top of a large paper clip and tie one end over the other to form a half hitch (or overhand) knot.

Gently tug the ends of the bow so that the middle knot is about ¾″ tall.

Finish the bow by using a glue gun to keep the fabric sitting at the top of the clip. Stick the nozzle of the glue gun inside the bow near the paper clip and squeeze a tiny bit of hot glue into the knot. Squeeze more glue into the side of the knot and quickly shape the bow so the fabric lies nicely.

Trim the bow ends to the length you desire (here, that is 1.25" from outside the knot to the trimmed edge).

Use a strip of washi tape on the Bible page where you'd like to place the bow clip to give the page more stability, if desired. Clip the bow on top.

SUPPLIES · SUPPLIES

- **Hot Glue Gun**
- **Large Gold Paperclip**
- **Coordinating Fabric**
- **We R Memory Keepers Teal TAB Punch**

WHAT I LEARNED FROM CRISTIN:

best tips | what I took away | things to try next time

date _____

SECTION 1:5

JILLIAN UNGERBUEHLER

HOSPITALITY: PERFECTION IS NOT THE POINT

REVELATION 3:20

I am journaling this entry alongside Revelation 3:20. In my small group Bible study we are learning about Biblical hospitality and what it looks like to open not only our homes but our hearts to others. I like to journal my takeaways to help me remember what I've learned. For this page I'm journaling about having a hospitable heart toward the Lord.

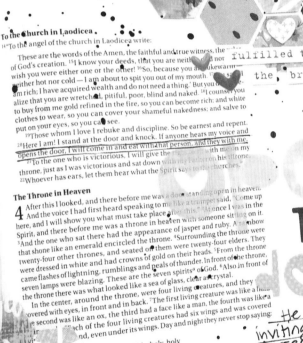

When Bible journaling, **THE VERY FIRST THING I DO** is figure out what idea I want to illustrate on my page.

WHAT DOES GOD WANT ME TO FOCUS ON DURING MY TIME IN HIS WORD THAT WILL STAY IN MY HEART AFTER MY BIBLE IS CLOSED?

After I've read the passage, looked to my study notes, and prayed, there is a title that typically jumps out at me.

In this case, **IT'S AN EXCERPT FROM THE VERSE ITSELF.**
I then like to make that phrase, or the main word from that phrase, become the focal point of my page.

Sometimes I make **THE TITLE THE LARGEST ELEMENT IN THE MARGIN,**
as was the case for this page. When flipping through my journaling Bible, you will see a lot of big and bold titles!

For this entry, I chose to use clear alphabet stamps to get the most meaningful word of the big idea down in the margin.

TECHNIQUE · TECHNIQUE

You could also use alphabet stickers or your own hand-lettering skills. When using clear stamps like these, an acrylic block and an ink pad are also needed. I like to use pigment ink because it is less likely to bleed through the thin Bible pages.

I peeled the alphabet letter stamps needed to spell the word "open" off of the stamp backer. One at a time I stuck each letter to the acrylic block, lightly pressed the stamp into the ink pad, and stamped the inked letter on the page. For large titles (like this one), I started by stamping the letters on the outer edge of the page and worked my way in. This ensured I would have enough room to stamp the whole word. In this case, I began with the letter *N* on the right edge and stamped the word backwards, letter by letter. Also, before beginning to stamp, it may be handy to write the word you're spelling on a scrap piece of paper so it isn't accidentally misspelled.

TECHNIQUE · TECHNIQUE

Side Tip: After stamping, you'll need to clean off any excess ink with a baby wipe before returning it to the stamp backer.

ASK ME HOW I LEARNED THIS.

From there, I used alphabet stickers to build the rest of my title before using a pen to underline and circle the passage. This keeps me from inadvertently covering it up with the additional elements I plan to add to my page.

- **Black Journaling Pen**
- **Homespun Alphabet Stamps**
- **Acrylic Block and Pigment Ink**
- **Tiny Colorful Alphabet Stickers**

SUPPLIES · SUPPLIES

WHAT COMES NEXT?
Cut Paper

After I have the title down on my page (or at least the idea in my head) I usually look around to see how I can best illustrate the idea in my margin. Unfortunately, I was not blessed with the gift of drawing, so a lot of times, I use stickers and other design elements to help me portray the passage.

TECHNIQUE · TECHNIQUE

In this case, I thought the best illustration to represent the passage would be an open door. And, since we all know I'm not the best at drawing, I chose to use a mosaic style patterned paper to...

To bring some fun patterns and extra color to the Bible margin, I punched hexagon shapes from several coordinating pieces of patterned paper. I also used a handheld squeeze punch to cut uniform hexagon shapes from the different papers.

Side Tip: You may want to cut more than what you will use so you can choose from the different patterns. In this case, I cut three times more hexagons than I intended to glue on my page so that I had a variety of colors and patterns to choose from.

TECHNIQUE · TECHNIQUE

Before adhering the hexagons to the page, keep these tips in mind:

- Lay them out on the page before committing to adhesive to make sure you like where they are placed.

- You may want to keep a small border in between each shape instead of gluing them down right next to each other, edge to edge.

In this case, I used a tape runner to put a small amount of adhesive on the back of each hexagon and clustered them in three places. I like to start at the top, move down to the bottom, and then create a small cluster in the middle, this time just under my title. This creates a visual triangle and moves your eye around the margin. It also comes in handy when placing those finishing touches to come. When placing the cut shapes on the page I like to make sure the color is evenly distributed. This means keeping two similar pink shades from living right next to each other. Instead, try adhering a teal or yellow in between them.

BONUS POINTS
for placing contrasting colors side by side as that makes the mosaic pop!

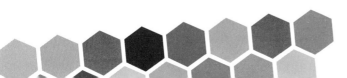

For me, the two most important elements on a Bible journaling page are the title and the handwritten journaling. With the title done and the patterned paper in place, I want to be sure to jot down a note about my prayerful response to this passage before moving on to anything else.

Church in Laodicea

he angel of the church in Laodicea write:

hese are the words of the Amen, the faithful and true witness, the ruler God's creation. ¹⁵I know your deeds, that you are neither cold nor hot. I sh you were either one or the other! ¹⁶So, because you are lukewarm — ither hot nor cold — I am about to spit you out of my mouth. ¹⁷You say, 'I n rich; I have acquired wealth and do not need a thing.' But you do not re- ize that you are wretched, pitiful, poor, blind and naked. ¹⁸I counsel you buy from me gold refined in the fire, so you can become rich; and white lothes to wear, so you can cover your shameful nakedness; and salve to ut on your eyes, so you can see.

¹⁹Those whom I love I rebuke and discipline. So be earnest and repent.
²⁰Here I am! I stand at the door and knock. If anyone hears my voice and opens the door, I will come in and eat with that person, and they with me. ²¹To the one who is victorious, I will give the right to sit with me on my throne, just as I was victorious and sat down with my Father on his throne. ²²Whoever has ears, let them hear what the Spirit says to the churches."

The Throne in Heaven

After this I looked, and there before me was a door standing open in heaven. And the voice I had first heard speaking to me like a trumpet said, "Come up here, and I will show you what must take place after this." ²At once I was in the Spirit, and there before me was a throne in heaven with someone sitting on it. ³And the one who sat there had the appearance of jasper and ruby. A rainbow that shone like an emerald encircled the throne. ⁴Surrounding the throne were twenty-four other thrones, and seated on them were twenty-four elders. They were dressed in white and had crowns of gold on their heads. ⁵From the throne came flashes of lightning, rumblings and peals of thunder. In front of the throne, seven lamps were blazing. These are the seven spirits of God. ⁶Also in front of the throne there was what looked like a sea of glass, clear as crystal.

In the center, around the throne, were four living creatures, and they covered with eyes, in front and in back. ⁷The first living creature was like a li... the second was like an ox, the third had a face like a man, the fourth was like a flying eagle. ⁸Each of the four living creatures had six wings and was cov... with eyes all around, even under its wings. Day and night they never stop sa...

" 'Holy, holy, holy
is the Lord God Almighty,'
who was, and is, and is to come

⁹Whenever the living creatures give glory, honor and thanks... m who sit the throne and who lives for ever and ever, ¹⁰the twenty-four ... fall dov before him who sits on the throne and worship him who lives for ... d eve They lay their crowns before the throne and say:

¹¹"You are worthy, our Lord and God,
to receive glory and honor and power,
for you created all things,
and by your will they were created
and have their being."

The Scroll and the Lamb

Then I saw in the right hand of him w... ing on both sides and sealed with se... claiming in a loud voice, "Who is wort...

THE DOOR

...e calls & knocks,
... us into
fellowship
Him ♡

Once I write my journal entry, I then look to see if there are any large spaces on the page that have been left blank. I give the page a once-over to see if any spots jump out at me. And, most the time, they do. I don't like for things to look too neat, and one way to break up all those straight lines is by splattering my page with a little paint and ink. Enter the black paint splatter.

I realize to some the thought of splattering black paint over your new entry may make you want to turn the page.

HEAR ME OUT!

I've found that with small black splatters, the paint can fill in some of those spaces that otherwise have nothing else going on. It also breaks up the "too neat" look of the page and creates some cohesion from one corner to the next.

Brush around the pan to pick up the color and then lightly tap the brush, about a third of the way down the barrel, on your index finger. The collision of paintbrush into finger makes the paint leap from the brush and land on the Bible page.

Side Tip: If you are still unsure of this method, perhaps try it out on a scrap piece of paper to practice controlling the paint splatter.

Once the paint is dry, I then add a few small embellishments and date stamp my entry to document when I created it.

- Water
- Date Stamp
- Ink Pad
- Small Paintbrush
- Black Watercolor Paint

best tips | what I took away | things to try next time

date _____

SECTION 1:6

THE RAINBOW OF HIS PROMISE

EZEKIEL 1:28

APRIL CROSIER

This passage has a beautiful description of how Ezekiel saw the glory of the Lord. Just like the beautiful rainbow of His promise in Genesis, we continue to see this icon play out throughout Biblical history. Being able to witness such a unique, natural symbol of promise in our day-to-day lives is so special to me. It's like a little whisper straight from God saying, "Hey April, I've got this! Don't you worry about a thing, it's all part of My plan." I can't wait for the day that I get to witness every OUNCE of God's glory in heaven...the rainbow to top all rainbows!

To start our base layer for this page,
I thought it would be perfectly fitting to add some

RAINBOWTIZED

goodness to our Bible margins as we

DIVE DEEP INTO THE BEAUTY OF THE LIKENESS OF THE GLORY OF GOD.

One of my absolute favorite "TRASH TREASURES" is bubble wrap

— I hoard it!

IT IS SUCH A FUN, YET UNASSUMING LITTLE TOOL TO USE IN OUR BIBLES IN CREATIVE WAYS.

For this particular project, I cut out a strip of bubble wrap to fit exactly into my space by measuring the length as well as width of my Bible margin and worked from those dimensions. A little imperfection is totally fine—no need to trim to exactness because we're allowed that margin of error, friends.

GOD'S GRACE IS EVIDENT EVEN HERE IN OUR MARGINS!

Once I had my margin-sized strip of bubble wrap, I went to gently brush down some acrylic paint in a rainbow pattern.

For a clean and gorgeous bubble-wrapped rainbow, the goal is to paint only the bubbles and as little of the in-between sections as possible. The catch is making sure that you add enough of the pigment that it doesn't dry out or show too thinly on your page. It's a fine line to balance, but you've got this!

Side Tip: Try to have soft hands! If you press your brush of color down too hard, you'll push color down between the air-filled bubbles.

Continue adding colors in your pattern until you have filled your strip of bubble wrap.

Very carefully, very slowly, very cautiously flip your painted bubble wrap piece over and align it from top to bottom with your Bible margin. Using your fingers, gently press each section down to transfer the color to your Bible page and once again—carefully, slowly, cautiously—peel the bubble wrap off the page and set aside or discard.

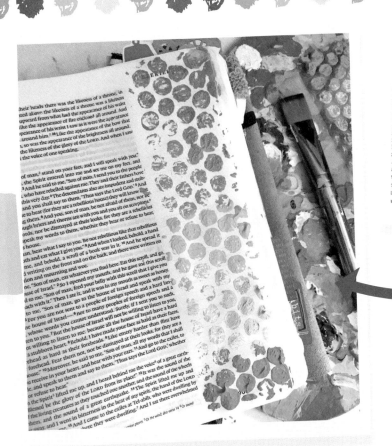

Admire your work, friend. Your bubble-wrapped rainbow Bible margin is absolutely gorgeous!

- **Bubble Wrap**
  [repurposed or new]
- **Acrylic Paints**
- **Paint Brush**

SUPPLIES SUPPLIES

Now that we have a beautiful base layer to work upon, I'm excited to dive into the main portion of the page with some chunky, layered paper pieces!

If you're anything like me, you may not be incredibly talented in lettering or freestyle drawing. So paper pieces already adorned with beautiful scripts and fonts, along with a handful of paper florals or geometrics, are totally my BFF.

I love the extra bit of dimension they give my Bible margin. With a few simple scissor snips or pen markings, it's easy to give them some extra "me-ness" for a more unique use in my own way!

For this project, I pulled two gorgeous pieces of paper ephemera from one of my favorite Illustrated Faith product lines that matched my bubble-wrapped paint palette. Once I glued these two pieces together, I placed them on my page—careful not to cover up my focus verse here in Ezekiel.

I added some wonky pen circles around the used-to-be chat bubble that I scissored down to help the paper piece POP up off the page visually.

I then added in some pretty little doodad pieces like the crosses and hearts to create a visual triangle that is super pretty to feast my eyes upon!

I have long learned that as fun and purposeful as our Bible margin art is, it's also incredibly beneficial to invest some margin space for thoughts or prayers as well. I'm careful to layer my paper pieces to allow for some good old-fashioned handwriting either above or below my main focal art piece, as you can see here! Just a few heartfelt words or a main takeaway blurb from a sermon is all you need to scribble down to remind yourself what you've learned in a specific passage. You'll be so thankful you did this come future days when you're flipping through a chunky, filled-up Bible of worship and seeing what all God has taught you!

SUPPLIES SUPPLIES

- **Illustrated Faith Paper Pieces and Sticker Sheet: All People All Nations**
- **Illustrated Faith Pen**
- **Illustrated Faith Glue Runner**
- **Enamel Hearts**

FINISHING TOUCHES:
How to Make Layered Tabs

OUR PAGE IS ALMOST DONE, FRIENDS!
We have a gorgeous, colorful base layer along with some beautiful art work to draw our eyes alongside our own personal journaling.
OUR FINAL STEP IS TO "SEAL THE DEAL" WITH SOME LAYERED TABBING!
This is one of my absolute FAVORITE techniques and I use it on every. single. page in my art worship Bible!

Creating a tab piece at the top [or side] of my Bible margins is important to me because it gives me a general idea of what that page is covering. Whether the topic is needing grace, gaining courage, or offering up praises, I can add a tab to my page and be able to see it from the outside of my Bible and flip right to what my heart needs to reread...like a little tab forest! And for my tab pieces, my motto is "the more the merrier"—layer it up!

To get started on a layered tab piece, I like to dig through my collection of tabbies that I keep stored in a cute little vintage tin. Alternatively, you could create your own tabs using cute scrapbook paper and a TAB punch or scissors! The sky is the limit!!

Here I've pulled out a small handful of color-coordinating tabbies that match my rainbow background and paper pieces. Play around with layering one on top of the other and piecing the tab collection together in different ways until you are pleased with the style.

Side Tip: At this point, you should always, always, always staple your tab collection together. If you unlayer them to glue each piece down to the others individually, you'll never find the exact same layout that brought you so much happiness. Trust me here, friends, add a staple.

Next, I want to add a little topic title to my layered tab section. This one that says "God's glory" is soooo perfect! I grabbed it out of my Illustrated Faith basics wordfetti booklet. And...voilà! A fabulous layered tab is now ready to glue down at the top of our completed page so we can quickly find and reference it later. Yes and amen, friends!

SUPPLIES

- Ephemera
- Tiny Attacher
- Tape Runner
- B&W Tabbies
  All People All Nations
- Basics Wordfetti Booklet

best tips | what I took away | things to try next time

date _____

SECTION 1:7

A SEASON OF WAITING

LLANET FERNANDEZ

JOB 34:21

This verse sets the tone of my current season. It reminds me that though I may be standing in the gap of where I've been and where I want to go, God sees me, He is with me. My season of waiting is intentional, like everything God does. I may not understand it, but I allow Him to work His wonder by simply trusting Him. This Scripture reminds me than even when things seem still, He is moving. God always looks out for us.

UNDER THE STARS

THE VERY FIRST THING I DID

was use Illustrated Faith's Digital Set from the Print and Pray Shop titled **"A GOD THAT SEES"** and print the set on a full sheet of clear sticker paper.

Another reason I'm drawn to Print and Pray sets are the Scripture references. I just love reading through all of them and identifying which one speaks to me and my season in life. It allows me to have a better foundation to ponder the Word and journal through it.

TECHNIQUE · TECHNIQUE

Side Tip: If you want more options/elements to journal with, there are also two additional coordinating sets that include cards and patterned paper. I printed both the card and paper set on 110 lb. white cardstock.

AS YOU BEGIN YOUR JOURNALING PROCESS, MAKE SURE THAT IT'S PERSONAL; THAT IS WHEN CREATIVITY BEGINS TO FLOW.

Now that I have chosen a verse, I've highlighted it by using the Illustrated Faith Precision Pen (no bleed-through) so that I can identify it on the page.

SO NOW, LET'S GET STARTED.

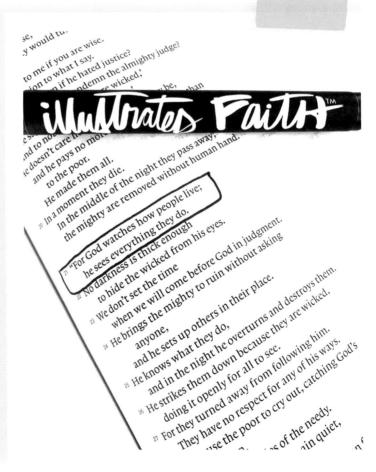

The first thing to do is read the verse to yourself and focus on the words that LEAP OUT of the page. These may trigger memories, people, even circumstances, so allow God to dig deep in your heart and see what He shows you and speaks to you as you read your verse. For me, the words that jumped out as I read my verse were WATCHES and SEES.

As I looked through my digital set for inspiration, the binoculars, word phrases, starry elements, and magnifying glass immediately caught my eye. The word phrase sticker here–

was the focus I wanted, so I chose to use it on the set as the main element on my page.

For someone like me, who is not good at lettering, these stickers really do the trick. Once you have chosen your main sticker, then decide placement. Highlighting my verse first helps me arrange the stickers on the page. You want to make sure to embellish your verse, so I'm going to anchor my page with this beautiful word sticker sentiment and place it next to the verse.

SUPPLIES ✂ **SUPPLIES**

- **Precision Scissors**
- **NLT Reflections Journaling Bible**
- **Illustrated Faith Precision Pen .65**
- **Avery 8163 Full Page Clear Sticker Paper**
- **Illustrated Faith: Print and Pray A God that Sees by Shawna Clingerman**

Next, cut out the remaining elements on your page to check for size, scale, and placement. Once cut, place them in different areas on the page to get a feel for the direction you want to go. Those starry binoculars have my heart so I want them to frame the word sticker I already placed on my page. Once done, it's important to see the scale of what is already on the page, so keep in mind that you'll need to leave space to write out your prayers.

NOW, LET'S WORK ON A HEADER.

I love tabs and flairs, they bring in some much-needed dimension to a page. My friends lovingly call this technique a "tab forest" simply because I just tend to layer several tabs and elements to make a big header on the page.

I started by printing out the coordinating patterned paper set on cardstock. I chose two or three (depending on how big I want to go) and punched the tabs with a scalloped puncher (this creates a cloud effect). Then, I layered both tabs and attached them with a tape runner (I don't adhere these to the page yet).

Next, I wanted to add a brad banner to the tabs I just layered. I attached it in the middle between both tabs by piercing through the paper with the metal clasp found in the back of the brad. Once that was done, I placed it aside. I wanted to add an element that goes outside the margins of the page, so I grabbed those *cute* binoculars. I placed the sticker onto a piece of cardstock to make it a little sturdier, cut it out, and attached it to the outer edge of the page, slightly edging out from the top and side page margin.

To the left of those binoculars I added the magnifying glass. I ran the tape runner only on the handle and placed it at a slight right angle to the left of the binoculars, having the glass portion pop out from the top margin. Last, I ran the tape runner to the back of my tabs and adhered it to the top of the page towards the left, allowing the right corner of the tab to overlap the middle of the handle of the magnifying glass.

TECHNIQUE · TECHNIQUE

It's always better to do the bulk of your layers towards the outside of the page, that way closing your Bible is easier. To finish off, I add a cute flair in between my tab and elements, and now my header is complete.

I finished off the page by adding a camper sticker on the bottom left corner and a tree and compass on the right to tie in the outdoor feel that I want.

Now for the best part:

WRITE IT OUT!!!!

I wrote God a little love note on the margin.

SUPPLIES · SUPPLIES

- **Tape Runner**
- **Brad: My Mind's Eye Wander Collection**
- **110 lb. White Cardstock**
- **Flair: Fancy Pants Design**
- **Fiskars Scalloped Edge Punch**
- **Illustrated Faith: Print and Pray A God that Sees Pattern Paper by Shawna Clingerman**

LET'S ADD A FUN TRANSLUCENT COVER.

I started by printing the starry paper of the patterned paper bundle on acetate/transparency paper. Then, I placed it on top of my Bible page by cutting it slightly smaller than the size of my page. To accentuate my cover, I then cut out the cluster of three trees found in the set. This cluster is on sticker paper, so I pasted it on to cardstock and cut it out. There is a matching set of the same cluster of trees on the card set, so I went ahead and cut those out in order to have two tree clusters.

Last, I cut out another card that has a cluster of trees with tents, which I will use as the main piece. The idea is to use the other two tree cluster pieces–one on each side. I centered the main piece (trees and tents) and ran the tape runner to secure it. I ran the tape only in the center and left the edges alone. Then, I got each remaining cluster of trees and ran the tape runner down the middle of each piece and slightly tucked each cluster behind the center piece (one on each side).

Side Tip:
You don't want it to overlap your page or cut it too small where you see large white page margins. Cut it where it sits inside the margins.

Last, I added the banner of Hide-and-Seek in the middle. When the cover was done, I cut a narrow piece of clear packing tape and placed it on the side of the cover closest to the spine. As I placed the cover over the page, I secured it with the tape, creating a hinge effect (like a door), and now it's done.

SUPPLIES

• Tape Runner
• 110 lb. White Cardstock
• Acetate/Transparency Paper
• Illustrated Faith: Print and Pray
  A God that Sees Cards by Shawna Clingerman

best tips | what I took away | things to try next time

date _____

GO FOR IT

TAKE TWO

SECTION 2

SECTION 2:1

BEING A MIRROR

SHANNA NOEL

MATTHEW 5:13-20

Now that we have had fun playing with scraping acrylic paint (see page 21), I wanted to show you another way to layer it up and have a little more control (don't worry it's equally fun, I promise!).

MATTHEW 5-6

BELIEVERS ARE SALT

13 "You are the salt of the earth. But if salt sh[...] for anything but to be thrown [...] and trample
15 16 [...] are the light of the world. A city situated on a hill cannot be hidden. No one lights a lamp and puts it un[...]t, but rather on a lampstand, and it gives [...] for all who are in the house. In the same way, let
16 you[...]e before others, so that they may see your good works and give glory to your Father in heaven.

CHRIST FULFILLS THE LAW

17 18 "Don't think that I came to abolish the Law or the Prophets. I did not come to abolish but to fulfill. For truly I
19 tell you, until heaven and earth pass away, not the smallest letter or one stroke of a letter will pass away from the law until all things are accomplished. Therefore, whoever breaks one of the least of these commands and teaches others to do the same will be called least in the kingdom of heaven. But whoever does and teaches
20 these commands will be called great in the kingdom of heaven. For I tell you, unless your righteousness surpasses that of the scribes and Pharisees, you will never get into the kingdom of heaven.

MURDER BEGINS IN THE HEART

21 "You have heard that it was said to our ancestors, **Do not murder**, and whoever murders will be subject
22 to judgment. But I tell you, everyone who is angry with his brother or sister will be subject to judgment. Whoever insults his brother or sister, will be subject to the court. Whoever says, 'You fool!' will be subject
23 to hellfire. So if you are offering your gift on the altar, and there you remember that your brother or sister
24 has something against you, leave your gift there in front of the altar. First go and be reconciled with your
25 brother or sister, and then come and offer your gift. Reach a settlement quickly with your adversary while you're on the way with him to the court, or your adversary will hand you over to the judge, and the judge
26 to the officer, and you will be thrown into prison. Truly I tell you, you will never get out of there until you have paid the last penny.

ADULTERY BEGINS IN THE HEART

27 28 "You have heard that it was said, **Do not commit adultery**. But I tell you, everyone who looks at a woman
29 lustfully has already committed adultery with her in his heart. If your right eye causes you to sin, gouge it
30 out and throw it away. For it is better that you lose one of the parts of your body than for your whole body to
31 be thrown into hell. And if your right hand causes you to sin, cut it off and throw it away. For it is better that you lose one of the parts of your body than for your whole body to go into hell.

DIVORCE PRACTICES CENSURED

31 32 "It was also said, **Whoever divorces his wife must give her a written notice of divorce**. But I tell you, everyone who divorces his wife, except in a case of sexual immorality, causes her to commit adultery. And whoever marries a divorced woman commits adultery.

TELL THE TRUTH

33 "Again, you have heard that it was said to our ancestors, **You must not break your oath, but you must
34 keep your oaths to the Lord.** But I tell you, don't take an oath at all: either by heaven, because it is God's
36 throne; or by the earth, because it is his footstool; or by Jerusalem, because it is the city of the great King. Do
37 not swear by your head, because you cannot make a single hair white or black. But let your 'yes' mean 'yes,' and your 'no' mean 'no.' Anything more than this is from the evil one.

GO THE SECOND MILE

38 39 "You have heard that it was said, **An eye for an eye and a tooth for a tooth**. But I tell you, don't resist an
40 evildoer. On the contrary, if anyone slaps you on your right cheek, turn the other to him also. As for the one
41 who wants to sue you and take away your shirt, let him have your coat as well. And if anyone forces you to
42 go one mile, go with him two. Give to the one who asks you, and don't turn away from the one who wants to borrow from you.

LOVE YOUR ENEMIES

43 44 "You have heard that it was said, **Love your neighbor** and hate your enemy. But I tell you, love your enemies
45 and pray for those who persecute you, so that you may be children of your Father in heaven. For he causes
46 his sun to rise on the evil and the good, and sends rain on the righteous and the unrighteous. For if you love,
47 those who love you, what reward will you have? Don't even the tax collectors do the same? And if you greet only your brothers and sisters, what are you doing out of the ordinary? Don't even the Gentiles do the same?
48 Be perfect, therefore, as your heavenly Father is perfect.

HOW TO GIVE

6 "Be careful not to practice your righteousness in front of others to be seen by them. Otherwise, you have no
2 reward with your Father in heaven. So whenever you give to the [...] sound a trumpet before you, as the hypocrites do in the synagogues and on the streets, to be appl[...] by people. Truly I tell you they have their reward. But when you give to the poor, don't let your left han[...] what [...] but right hand is doing, so
3 th[...] your giving [...] be in secret. And your Father who sees in s[...] reward you

[...]W TO PRAY [...]henever you pray, you must not be like the [...] crites, because they love to [...] y standing in the synag[...] [...]n the [...] ners to be seen by peo[...] rly I tell you, they have their reward. But when you p[...] [...]o your [...] om, shut your door, and [...] to your Father who is in secret, And your Father who [...] secret will [...] [...]ou. When you pray, don[...] b[...]ble like the Gentiles, since they imagine they'll be h[...] their many [...] [...]n't be like them, because your Father knows the things you need before you ask [...]

Help me Be an example of... YOU

Thank you JESUS For the wonderful Example you give us through your word, actions love + grace. Help me to be an Example of those to tell PEOPLE you place in my life thru Heart amen

FIRST DECIDE ON YOUR COLOR PALETTE. THERE'S LOTS OF WAYS TO PICK YOUR PALETTE!

1. Pick colors that make you happy!

2. Find a card, an art piece, or your favorite outfit and pull colors from that.

3. Pinterest is a wonderful source for all things color! Grab some inspiration from there!

NOW THAT YOU HAVE YOUR COLORS PICKED OUT, GRAB A COUPLE PAINT BRUSHES (I LIKE TO USE FLAT-EDGE PAINT BRUSHES FOR SOMETHING LIKE THIS) AND SOME BABY WIPES.

Start with one of your lighter colors, loading up your brush with some paint, and bring it to your page. As you apply the paint to the page, be aware of what size marks you are wanting to make. If you "mess up," don't worry; we are adding lots of layers and you won't even notice at the end. The first color is the most important of the pattern because you are setting the blueprint, or foundation, for the colors. All the other colors you apply after this will play along this same pattern. You can see I started off with a triangle across the page and then will follow with each color in that same pattern, building layers and playing with that triangle I have created.

When you are ready, try doing this same technique with a baby wipe. Wrap the baby wipe around your finger and then apply a little bit of paint on it and make those same marks with your new color, following that pattern you have already set for yourself!

FUN, RIGHT?

Pro Tip:
If you find that you cover the words too much and are no longer able to read them, take the baby wipe (while the paint is still wet) and gently wipe some away so you can see the words again! See, I told you! Baby wipes to the rescue again!

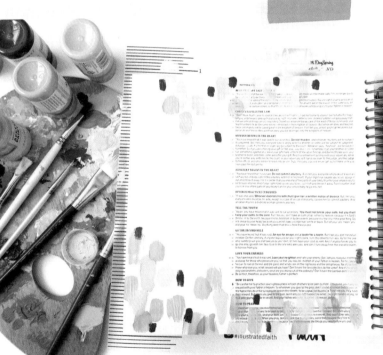

Keep repeating this process until you have used all the colors you want. Play with different size strokes and brushes to create some fun variation in your pattern.

- **Acrylic Paint**
- **Baby Wipes**
- **Paint Brushes**
- **Paint Palette**
- **Bible Mat**

Once you are done, step away and look at your beautiful page and allow it to fully dry before you move on to step two!

When Bible journaling, there are times when God puts a strong message in my heart—a powerful message that doesn't require a lot of words. In these moments, it helps just to have a big ole, heart-pumping, soul-pouring title that sums it all up!

AND THAT IS OKAY!

Remember, there are no rules here! You may even find some pages that require zero journaling or words because the photo, illustration, or color says it all.

For this page, I wanted to use a large title in place of journaling so I pulled out the clear stickers from the Illustrated Faith Basics line. I love clear stickers because they melt into the pages and allow the colors underneath to peek through, especially with these striking black-and-white images. My sticker reads

"HELP ME TO BE AN EXAMPLE OF ..."

which is a wonderful journaling prompt! I love that this really allows you to take it in so many directions and customize it for your specific journaling needs.

For this journaling entry, I wanted it to read...

Help me to be an example of...
YOU.

So, I used a mix and match of leftover alphas (*my favorite look!*) to complete my journaling/title for this page. I added this little panda here as I think it is such a cute illustration of reaching up to God (at least that is how I am using him here). Super simple and tells exactly what I am wanting to remember from this Bible passage.

As you work on big titles to help you tell the whole story, keep in mind what you are going to want to remember when you flip back to this page.

Is it a prayer? • Is it a statement of gratitude?
Is it a quote from your pastor?

Write all those things down,
this is a perfect place to do that!

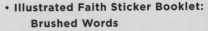

- **Illustrated Faith Sticker Booklet: Brushed Words**
- **Daiso Panda**

We talked a little about art marks (26-27) and how fun they are to bring a page together. This time we are going to take it a step further and

PLAY WITH SOME DIFFERENT MEDIUMS!

Instead of placing my art marks on the outside of the paint base we created earlier, this time I am going to use the paint marks to contain my art marks (for the most part, remember this is all about breaking the rules!). I am also going to use the art marks to set the colors, so where there is a light blue I might use a darker blue over it to create art marks!

I will also be using different mediums to create the art marks. Let's break out all of our fun supplies!

Supplies to try with this method: pens, crayons, pencils, stamps with art marks, brush pens, paint, ripped washi tape, stencils, white paint pens,

YOU NAME IT!

What we are looking for here are colors that go with the paint layer we have already created!
Once you have gathered your supplies, follow the blueprint you have already created with the paint, adding blue hash marks over the light blue paint, or dark pink hearts over the light pink, for example. Again, this is something that you can play around with and can get a feel for your personal style. Feel free to try it here in the workbook or on a scratch piece of paper, and when you feel comfortable move into your Bible.

Don't feel like you can't move outside the paint blueprint you created for yourself! I just suggest starting there and then go wild and have fun with it! One of my favorite things to do in this part of the process is to rip up washi tape to add to the pattern, again sticking with the same colors or adding in some black-and-white washi tape for a fun contrast. I typically make the washi strips around the same size as the paint marks for a really fun look!

- **Neocolors II**
- **Acrylic Paint**
- **White Paint Pen**
- **Faber-Castell Big Brush Pens**
- **Illustrated Faith Journaling Pens**
- **Illustrated Faith Washi Tape: Black and White Criss Cross**

PRACTICE HERE!

SECTION 2:2

ROOTED IN FAITH

COLOSSIANS 2:6-7 ESV

ELAINE DAVIS

I'm a learner and a dreamer, but I also struggle with change. It's like I want to go and do all these new things, but I want everything to stay the same. What!? That makes no sense at all! But I'm a human and I'm imperfect. My heart has flawed logic. But that's where faith comes in! I want to grow, but I need help doing it. I need help feeling okay about whatever changes may come. Colossians 2:6-7 ESV says: "Therefore, as you received Christ Jesus the Lord, so walk in Him, rooted and built up in Him and established in the faith, just as you were taught, abounding in thanksgiving." So even if we fear change or fear what's to come, if we are rooted in our faith we will come through it with gratitude on the other side.

I found this verse to be incredibly timely for me because change has been a big factor in my life the past year. Not just tiny changes, BIG MILESTONE CHANGES! But I am here and I am grateful to the Faithful One for bringing me to it and through it!

For the base of this page, I wanted something bright but soft-handed. One of my favorite techniques for applying paint is something I came up with a couple of years ago. I hate washing out brushes so I'm always looking for new ways to apply paint that are disposable. Enter the Baby Wipe Technique! I fold a standard baby wipe into a pointed shape around my finger and apply a small amount of paint directly to the wipe, about half the size of a pea. Then I start swiping the baby wipe across the page (usually vertically) just like I'm finger painting. The wetness of the wipe gives the paint a creamy application with no brush strokes in it! It also works great for blending colors.

For this page, I used the same baby wipe to apply four different colors without heat setting the colors in between. By NOT heat setting each color, it gives you a wonderful blended look with your colors instead of a stark contrast. After finishing the paint, you can use a heat tool to set it, or let it air dry.

Step two of this piece is adding some interest and layers to the background. This was easily accomplished using a wood block flower stamp and a black permanent ink pad. Stamping your image off the edge of the page gives the illusion that your items have movement instead of a full image floating in the middle of the paper. It frames the Scripture nicely!

The last component of the page's foundation is some die cuts. I wanted to bring something bright to the foreground because this project centered around growth reminds me of bright, sunny weather! These cheery flowers and leaves made the perfect addition, and they're super simple to apply with a glue stick or an adhesive runner!

SUPPLIES

- Baby Wipes
- Heat Tool
- StazOn Ink Pad: Jet Black
- Tombow Mono Dots Adhesive
- Illustrated Faith Bible Mat
- Liquitex Basics Acrylic Paint:
  Light Blue Violet
- Liquitex Heavy Body Acrylic Paint:
  Medium Magenta
- Master's Touch Acrylic Paint:
  Purple Red & Titanium White
- Bella Blvd Ephemera Pack: Island Escape
- Stampendous Wood Block Stamp: Fresh Bloom

One of the things I'm known for in my art is using what I like to call **"NONTRADITIONAL PRODUCTS,"** AKA **scraps and trash.**
It's such a great way to stretch your supplies, challenge yourself as an artist, and recycle!
Some everyday disposable items I've used in my pages in the past are:
BARCODES, TICKETS, GUM WRAPPERS, CLOTHING TAGS, BITS OF CARDBOARD CEREAL BOXES, JUNK MAIL, ENVELOPES, FRUIT STICKERS, POSTAGE STAMPS, TISSUE PAPER, AND MORE!
Most of these items you could find around your house or even in your junk drawer. I find beauty in the most uncommon places.

That said, I wanted to try something new on this page:
MAKING A POCKET OUT OF A SEED PACKET!

This will be the main part of my page and create extra room for my journaling underneath. I sewed some cute snippets on the outside of the seed packet to dress it up, including a ruffle made from party crepe paper. For the insert in the pocket, I grabbed a simple manila shipping tag from my stash and had some fun making it scrappy and happy! On the back of the seed packet, I glued down a 3x4 card from a Bella Blvd cut-apart paper.

To attach my seed packet, I used some washi tape to adhere one side of it to the edge of my Bible page. By placing half the washi width on the packet, I was able to wrap the other half around the edge of the page. This creates a little hinge so you can lift the packet like a door.

SUPPLIES

- Seed Packet
- 1" Circle Punch
- Manila Tag
- Ticket Stub
- Paper Scraps
- Green Crepe Paper
- Solid Washi Tape
- Sew-ology Thread Spool
- Bella Blvd 12x12 Paper Pack: Island Escape
- Illustrated Faith Alpha Stamps: Less Hustle More Jesus

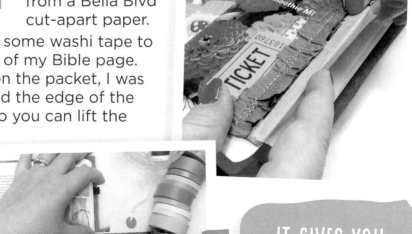

IT GIVES YOU SO MUCH SPACE FOR JOURNALING!

When I painted the background, I left the top left portion of the page open to give myself room for a title. Sometimes I just start a page and go with the flow, but other times I think ahead and leave myself some space for certain design elements. I mixed up some green dimensional alphas to give this page some variety. This is such a great way to just have some FUN with your title! If you run out of a letter in one kind of alpha, throw in another kind with it to make it fun and scrappy! These pages don't have to be the definition of "perfect" in order to connect you with God. On that note, I also wanted to highlight my verse in some way, so an art pen came in handy!

After giving some throwaway bits new life by putting them on my Bible page, I thought a little sparkle wouldn't hurt. I used some Stickles, archival safe glitter glue, to add a little shine. This is one of my favorite finishing touches to add a real pop to my projects! It just finishes it up with a sparkly treatment you can't beat!

TRY AND FROWN WHEN YOU'RE ADDING GLITTER TO ART— I'LL BET YOU CAN'T DO IT! ;)

I clustered some dimensional embellishments on my seed packet and in the upper right corner to draw your eye around the page and lead you to pulling out that tag. Don't forget the cherry on top—a date stamp! Adding a date is an important step to mark your work at a certain point in your life.

You or even your children will love looking back on these works of art, knowing exactly what point in your life you were working through it!

THESE ROOTS YOU'RE ESTABLISHING WILL LAST FOR GENERATIONS TO COME!

• Illustrated Faith Words Cardstock: Stick Booklet
• Bella Blvd Puffy Heart Stickers: Bell Pepper Mix
• Faber-Castell Big Brush Pen: Dark Naples Ochre
• Bella Blvd Wonky Alpha Puffy Stickers: Pickle Juice
• Bella Blvd Sticky Mix Cardstock Stickers: Island Escape
• Illustrated Faith Basics Epoxy Hexies: Apple of My Eye

• Illustrated Faith Pen
• UniBall Signo Pen in White
• Pickle Juice Mix & Punch Mix
• American Crafts Thickers in Eclair
• Illustrated Faith Date It Rotary Stamp
• Stickles by Ranger: Diamond & Yellow

SUPPLIES · SUPPLIES

PRACTICE HERE!

SECTION 2:3

PRODUCING GOOD FRUIT

HEATHER GREENWOOD

GALATIANS 5:22-23

I love Illustrated Faith's Fruit of the Spirit Collection. It inspired me to really think about and meditate on the fruits for the first time. Galatians 5:22-23 is a well-known verse that I've heard many times in my life; however, I've somehow managed not to really spend any time breaking down exactly what the verse means to me. I'm so grateful to have the Holy Spirit within me, working in me to produce good fruit.

A fun way to get paint down on the page and let loose is to

smash paint onto your page.

I'm going to use watered down acrylic paint
but you can do this with watercolors too.

First, we will pick two to three colors. I picked colors that coordinate with the collection I'm using. I would stick to lighter colors since this is not a controlled technique.

TECHNIQUE · TECHNIQUE

Also, try to stick to colors that would blend nicely together and not get muddy since they will be mixing together in areas. Usually I stick to colors that are both warm or both cold, but this time decided to use a pinky peach and light blue, making sure not to muddy up the colors too much.

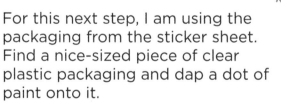
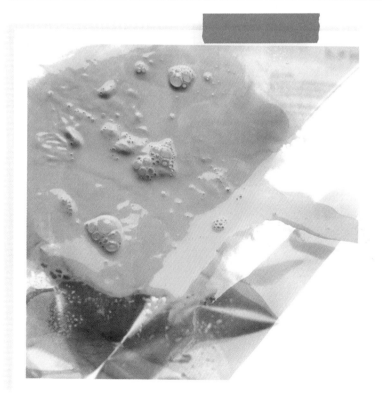

For this next step, I am using the packaging from the sticker sheet. Find a nice-sized piece of clear plastic packaging and dap a dot of paint onto it.

AS ALWAYS HAPPENS, I ENDED UP DROPPING THE CONTAINER OF PAINT AND SO I HAD MORE THAN JUST A DOT. WHEN THINGS LIKE THAT HAPPEN, I LAUGH IT OFF AND THANK GOD FOR REMINDING ME TO FOCUS ON THE WORSHIP AND NOT WORRY ABOUT PERFECTION. AFTER ALL, THIS TECHNIQUE IS VERY RANDOM AND ALL ABOUT LETTING GO OF CONTROL.

After we've added some paint to the packaging, we'll spray it with a couple sprays of water to water it down. Then we grab the packaging and smoosh the paint and water together to mix it up.

THIS IS WHERE THE FUN COMES IN...

Now smash it on your Bible pages in a few different places. The page is going to curl up from being so wet. Be careful when your page is so wet not to tear it. When it's that wet, it becomes very fragile.

Now we're going to repeat with our second color. I wiped off the packaging before starting the new color since I didn't want to mix the pink and blue too much. If I was using another warm color I would have kept the old paint on and added the new color over it for some fun mixing and blending. Have fun smashing paint until you are happy with your background.

Before we move on to the next step, make sure your page is dry first. I like to use a heat tool to dry quickly. This also helps to get some of the wrinkles out.

- **Packaging from Illustrated Cardstock Stickers: Faith Fruit of the Spirit**
- **Illustrated Faith Bible Mat**
- **ESV Journaling Bible**
- **Acrylic Craft Paint**
- **Water Spray Bottle**
- **Embossing Heat Tool**

WHAT COMES NEXT?
Mark Making with Stamps

One of my favorite things to do is to find things around the house that make for fun stamping.
I ALSO LIKE TO STAMP WITH PAINT AND NOT ALWAYS INK.
I found some
BUBBLE WRAP, CARDBOARD TUBES, AND A PENCIL ERASER
to stamp with on this page.

Bubble Wrap: Using your finger or a paint brush, smear some paint onto the bubble wrap lightly.

TECHNIQUE · TECHNIQUE

You don't want to get the paint in between the bubbles so just light strokes will work. Then smash it lightly onto your page randomly. Don't smash too hard and pop your bubbles; though the popping is fun, it will be a mess on your page. Just kiss it down like you're kissing someone's cheek.

Cardboard Tube: Using your finger, swipe some paint on the end of the tube and stamp it down. You can have fun with this one. You can turn the tube around and get some fun swirls, or just kiss it and get what looks like coffee cup stains. I stuck to odd numbers around the page and built three sections of mark making.

Pencil Eraser: Dip the eraser end into some paint and stamp it down on your page. It's like you're adding confetti to your page.

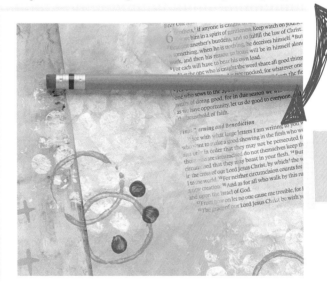

Lastly, I wanted to add some orange onto the page since there is orange in the collection. I grabbed the cute star stamps and stuck them to my acrylic block. I found an orange ink that matched the collection, tapped the stamp lightly onto the stamp pad, then kissed it onto the page. I kept to the three sections I had established with the other stamping.

- **Illustrated Faith Acrylic Paint Set**
- **Assorted Other Craft Paints**
- **Bubble Wrap**
- **Cardboard Tube**
- **Unused Pencil**
- **Illustrated Faith Stamp Set: Fruit of the Spirit**
- **Mememto LUXE Morocco Ink Pad**
- **Illustrated Faith Acrylic Stamp Block**

SUPPLIES · SUPPLIES

This time, instead of using a paper piece title, I wanted to mix some alphabet stickers to create a title. I picked out alphabet colors that matched the collection.

TECHNIQUE · TECHNIQUE

Mixing alphabet styles is lots of fun too. Using a different style for each word was fun to decide on. I like to use smaller alphabets to create the longer words. I also like taller alphabets to use for the word(s) I really want to stick out. This is your reminder to let go of perfection and have some fun placing the letters out of alignment and crooked.

I was going to highlight the verses but the marker was too bright so I grabbed some thin "highlighter" washi tape to highlight the verses. This is probably my favorite way to highlight a verse: highlighter washi!

After I highlighted the verse and added my title, I layered on the ephemera, stickers, and tabs. I picked out three of the smaller fruit pieces and the leaves to layer at the bottom. I also love the sentiment on the tab, that's really my prayer for these verses, that the Holy Spirit would guide me and produce fruit in me. Layering a sticker underneath it is a fun way to add some more color and texture. Then I tore apart the hexagons from the border sticker to add little hexagons all over.

Lastly, I added in some journaling and stamped a date. Normally, I stamp the date at the bottom, but there was no space on the bottom and lots of space right above the title.

I don't know why but I love stamping the date three times on top of each other. It feels like an added element to the page.

PLUS, IT DOESN'T ALWAYS STAMP PERFECTLY, SO AT LEAST I'LL HAVE ONE DATE I CAN SEE THAT TURNED OUT.

SUPPLIES SUPPLIES

- StazOn Ink Pad
- Illustrated Faith Pen Set
- Bella Blvd Wonky Alphabet
- Illustrated Faith Date-It Stamp
- Illustrated Faith Genesis Collection
- Illustrated Faith Highlighter Washi Tape
- Illustrated Faith Ephemera and Cardstock: Stickers Fruit of the Spirit

PRACTICE HERE!

SECTION 2:4

IF WE SEEK, WE WILL FIND

CRISTIN HOWELL

LUKE 11:9-10

I recently asked the Lord for insight and He answered me. This brought the passage in Luke 11:9-10 to mind. Jesus said if we ask, we receive, and if we seek, we will find. I have such joy that the Lord will answer us when we seek Him! It's my prayer that I will persistently seek Him with my whole heart, and that's what this page is about–a heart that seeks Jesus.

For this page, I wanted to use the Illustrated Faith Highlighter Washi to highlight my Scripture passage. Once again, highlighting the passage

keeps me focused on where I'm at and keeps the space clear.

I know I'm going to use a lot of alpha stickers, so I needed to stake out the Scripture first so I don't accidentally cover my passage.

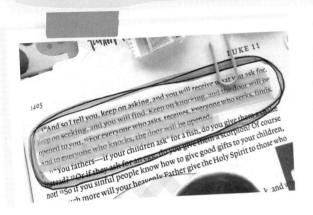

The Highlighter Washi is such a great product because it's sheer enough to see the Scripture underneath and it's exactly the right size to highlight the Bible text neatly. If uneven marker highlights frustrate you, then you will appreciate this.

Normally, I apply the washi directly over the words. This time, I'm first highlighting the Scripture with a marker and applying the washi in the space between the lines, in the white space. There is some overlap, but overall I like the solid text block this creates, and it completely covers up any uneven highlighter markings. I think this could be cute using contrasting colors, also.

Next, I used my Illustrated Faith pen and messy-circled the text. I purposely looped around the text loosely so the lines intersected. Then I filled in the loops with marker. I like how this creates a definite focused verse section. A rectangle or box or even a zig-zag outline would totally look cute to highlight a section.

TECHNIQUE · TECHNIQUE

If any of the highlighter washi pops up on the ends, I dab a glue stick on the edge and press it down. I like to use the corner of a paint card to burnish the washi onto the text so that the text is completely visible and is adhered permanently. Once you do this step, you will not be able to remove the washi without tearing the paper.

SUPPLIES · SUPPLIES

- Illustrated Faith Pen
- Kirarina 2Win Pen #013
- Illustrated Faith Highlighter Washi
- Faber-Castell Pitt Artist Pen Big Brush #131 Medium Flesh

For this page, I'm using digital printables from the Print and Pray Shop for my embellishments along with a sheet of digital paper. All of my embellishments are on a white cardstock. I printed them on clear sticker paper and then applied them to a sheet of white cardstock. Printing them this way means they can be used as a sticker or as a die cut.

Using a digital product means you'll never run out of an element you love. For instance, the hearts in this set are too cute, and I've printed extras. I cut out the hearts and girl studying her Bible, leaving a small white border around so that it looks like an actual manufactured die cut. I'm going to layer the embellishments and paper together to assemble my page. I love the look of several embellishments grouped together.

In the Print and Pray Shop, there are many digital papers to choose from, and sometimes the artist will create coordinating papers for their sets. This time I'm mixing and matching with the blue gingham.

I wanted to create circles (similar to the oval highlight section) so I found a jar lid measuring 3.75" to trace for the main circular backdrop.

The other circles are punched out using circle punches 1" and 1.25" in diameter.

The reason I added the circles is that not only does it add an extra layer of interest and pattern, but with all of the embellishments going on in this page, it needed a little something to keep the Bible study girl from looking too cluttered next to the alphas. Slipping a subtle background print underneath the girl created a separate visual grouping so that the eye can travel from the verse to the title to the girl. I cut out all the pieces and assembled them together, layering the Bible study girl on top of the blue gingham. Then, layering in all the hearts!

THERE'S SO MUCH TO LOOK AT!

SUPPLIES

- **Circle Punches: 1" & 1.25"**
- **Print and Pray Shop: Bible Bookworm**
- **Patterned Paper Bundle by Elaine Davis**
- **Print and Pray Shop: Rainbow Crush Alpha Set by Shanna Noel**
- **Print and Pray Shop: Cozy Up with the Good Book by Tamara Arcilla**

FINISHING TOUCHES:
Top It with A Bow

I hope I never get tired of tying bows onto my pages! I love looking through my fabric stash to find a cute fabric with all the colors I'm using in the page.

IT'S LIKE FINDING THE PERFECT PAIR OF EARRINGS FOR YOUR OUTFIT.

There are so many different ways to add bows to your page. I like to tie them onto paper clips and clip them onto the page, and I also like to punch holes into embellishments and tie bows onto the actual embellishments. I like bows on the top of the page and on the sides of the page. The bow I'm using here is similar to the ones you would tie when you're lacing up your shoes, but with the first overhand knot step left out.

When tying a bow for decorative use, I leave out the initial overhand knot to cut down on bulk. And since I glue the bows to the clips, the initial step to secure the fabric to the clip is not necessary. First cut a single strip of fabric (or use ribbon) 1.5" x 12" long. You can trim the ends later.

Thread the fabric strip through the end of a paper clip and center the paper clip in the middle of the strip. For this bow I used a smaller sized clip. On one side of the clip, form a loop and pinch it with your right thumb and forefinger.

With your left hand, wrap the other side of the strip around the loop and pull through to make a bow. Pretend you're tying your shoes but you're only doing the loop part.

Adjust the bow so that the printed sides of the fabric face outward and use a hot glue gun to secure the bow to the clip. Trim the edges.

SUPPLIES · SUPPLIES

TECHNIQUE · TECHNIQUE

• **Small Paper Clips**
• **Coordinating fabric 1.5" x 12"**

If bow tying is more than you want to take on, I have something even easier for you, but just as cute. Take a scrap of ribbon or fabric, and fold in half to make a *V* so the ends of the ribbon do not overlap. Then, staple the scrap onto the top of the page or onto the tab.

PRACTICE HERE!

SECTION 2:5

A BEAUTIFUL PICTURE OF GOD

JILLIAN UNGERBUEHLER

LUKE 15:11-32

For this entry, I decided to journal in Luke 15:11-32 where Jesus tells the parable of the prodigal son. I was struck by a quote my pastor shared in a sermon and wanted to include it here as this passage paints a beautiful picture of God as a loving Father.

color theory.

28524

LUKE 15:32 | 1185

you are loved

god the father

an infinitely powerful & intensely personal spiritual parent

homespun
CARDSTOCK STICKERS
A PERCENTAGE OF SALES FROM THIS PRODUCT WILL BE DONATED

OH MY HEA

God's big love

@illustratedfaith
#illustratedfaith

DaySpring

I started with a 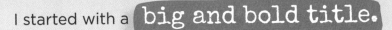 **big and bold title.**

I don't have the knack for hand lettering (AND THAT'S OKAY!)
so I look to craft supplies to help me with my large titles.
This time I used alphabet stickers to spell out the phrase I wanted to focus on.

AND INSTEAD OF PULLING OUT PART OF THE PASSAGE,
I USED A TITLE THAT CONVEYS THE MEANING OF THE PARABLE.

I already had a good idea which color scheme I would use for step two in my process, and that helped me decide which color alphabet stickers I would use for the title. To give a fun and playful look, I chose to select a variety of different size, font, and color alphabet stickers. I stuck with a short phrase for my title, this time

"GOD THE FATHER"

I also used a brushed word sticker and wordfetti stickers in coordinating colors to help finish off the title.

Before placing the alphabet sticker to the page, I lined up the letter stickers on the top edge of a Bible mat, leaving the top half of the stickers hanging over the edge. This helped me see where they would fit and look best in the margin. Once I settled on their placement I pressed the top half of the sticker down on the Bible page and gently pulled the Bible mat toward me until the sticker released. Then I firmly pressed the alphabet stickers down on the page so they wouldn't move around or fall off.

To make sure the whole word fit, I started spelling my word from the outer edge of the page and worked my way in. I then used my journaling pen to circle the passage I was focusing on and moved on to step two.

SUPPLIES

- Bible Mat
- Journaling Pen
- Alphabet Stickers
- Brushed Word Stickers
- Words Sticker Book

Next, I used patterned paper to create a fun background in the margin of my page. This time, I opted for a less uniform shape by hand cutting different-sized triangles from several sheets of coordinating patterned papers. I also chose to include more solid color pieces to help break up the bold patterns. This shape was a bit trickier to cohesively piece together because each triangle was a different size with different angles. Again, I chose to leave a small border between the shapes to get a mosaic look.

If you'll notice, I was careful to keep similar colors from sitting right next to each other, but I made sure that no two similar patterns were near each other. This made for a lot of shifting pieces around. I also noted the patterns that had a direction to them, like stripes for instance. If the stripes were oriented vertically on one triangle, I made sure to keep the stripes horizontal on the next triangle I adhered to the page.

Just like before, I used a tape runner on the back of each triangle to adhere it to the Bible page. Instead of clustering the hand-cut shapes in three places on the page to form a visual triangle, I opted to create one large triangle from several little ones. I love how this one large triangle really draws your eye to the passage. And the tactile yet relatively mindless process is a great way to meditate on the passage. Because Bible journaling isn't really about the pretty page at the end, it's about spending quality time with the Lord in His Word.

THE ART IS JUST A FUN BONUS!

SUPPLIES SUPPLIES

- Patterned Paper
- Scissors
- Tape Runner

To finish off the page, I took my pen and wrote a little quote in the margin of my journaling Bible that my pastor shared in a recent sermon. In my last entry I shared how I added black paint splatters on my page as a finishing touch. And if you just cannot bring yourself to try the same in your Bible, I have a fun alternative that will give a similar look:

STAMPING!

I used a clear stamp set with small patterns to create the look of black ink on the page. I mounted the clear stamp I wanted to use on an acrylic block. Then I lightly tapped the stamp onto the black pigment ink pad and pressed the stamp onto my Bible page. In a pinch, if you find yourself without an acrylic block, you can easily use the lid of the ink pad to mount the clear stamp on.

For a crisp stamp impression be sure to use a Bible mat underneath the paper.

If the stamping goes awry, please do not be discouraged! I have been known to, on more than one occasion, drop a fully inked stamp onto my page.

Once my stamping was done I then added a few more embellishments. I clustered enamel hearts in coordinating colors with wordfetti stickers on top of the black ink. The fun wordfetti phrases help drive home the overall theme of the page: God is our loving and perfect spiritual parent.

ONCE I HAD COMPLETED MY JOURNALING AND FINAL TOUCHES I AGAIN ADDED A DATE STAMP TO REMEMBER WHEN THE ENTRY WAS COMPLETED.

SUPPLIES

- Wordfetti
- Date Stamp
- Acrylic Block
- Black Ink Pad
- Enamel hearts
- Elements Stamp Set

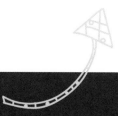

SECTION 2:6

GOD HAS A GREAT PURPOSE FOR ME

ROMANS 8:28

Romans 8:28 is a promise I hold close to my heart, knowing that God has a great purpose for me and that no matter what, **I am called by Him.**

APRIL CROSIER

For this Bible margin entry, I wanted to use my previous technique of painting with **BUBBLE WRAP** because it's seriously so addicting to play with....

BUT I KNEW I WANTED SOMETHING A LITTLE DIFFERENT.

First off, I laid down a couple of swipes of different tonal acrylic paint colors. No rhyme or reason here, friends—just quick swipes with pretty paints. This is a super easy technique for anyone to "master" because there's really no wrong way to dab a paint brush on a page.

TRUST ME HERE, OKAY?

TECHNIQUE · TECHNIQUE

I made sure to give each layer adequate time to dry between color layers and just played around with different hues until I had nearly filled the entire margin with color. The sky is the limit here—go with pink and purple like me, or maybe a variety of blues for an ocean theme...or add all the colors you can get your hands on for another rainbow margin! The fun part about this technique is that you can go as light or as dark in hue as you want...because we're about to add our bubble wrap goodness and really change it all up!

ONCE ALL OF MY BASE PAINT HAD DRIED REALLLLLLLY WELL,

I layered some titanium white acrylic paint thickly on a little scrap piece of bubble wrap that was left over from my rainbow page—being careful to only paint on the actual raised bubble portions, just like before. I then flipped the bubbles over and gently patted the paint covered swatch over multiple areas of my pre-painted background until I was satisfied with the coverage. The paint will last on the bubble wrap for multiple presses, so don't worry about needing to add more pigment.

JUST BUBBLE IT UP!

Using this specific technique of reverse bubble wrap painting gives me the option to use some really rich, dark colors on my page but still have the ability to lighten it up enough to journal on top of. The white bubbly look makes for a perfect place to pen my prayers and thoughts with just a hint of color peeking through from behind.

SUPPLIES · SUPPLIES

- Acrylic Paints
- Paint Brush
- Bubble Wrap
  [repurposed or purchased new]

WHAT COMES NEXT?
Creating a Layered Paper Piece Tip-In

This verse found here in

Romans 8 is so very good,

CHOCK-FULL OF TRUTH

in just one short sentence.
I knew I would need a good portion
of my Bible margin to journal

A PRAYER OF THANKSGIVING AND PRAISE TO GOD

for His love for little old me.
but I couldn't just go without some pretty art to look at too!

I grabbed up some favorite pieces from the Illustrated Faith All People All Nations tip-in collection in my absolute favorite colors for some layering fun. I happened to spy a shiny gold foil mini doily poking out from my craft cart as well, so I grabbed that cutie up too.

Just like we played around with piecing together our layered tab piece (see page 70-71), I did the same with these larger pieces of paper ephemera until I found a style I was happy with. I used my mini stapler to get it all connected and then trimmed down the doily to have a straight edge to align with the paper edge.

After adding some alpha stickers to my layered paper piece tip-in to show a quick expression of what sentiment I'm journaling about, I used a small piece of washi tape to adhere the tip-in piece to my Bible page. This is super easy to do, friends. Simply position your washi tape on the tip-in itself, using about half the width of the tape. With the other half of the width, you'll affix it directly on your Bible page so that you can flip it back and forth.

SUPPLIES

- **Mini Doily**
- **Tiny Attacher**
- **Washi Tape**
- **Homespun Alphas**
- **Tip-Ins: All People All Nations**

TECHNIQUE

Using a tip-in technique frees up so much margin space for heartfelt journaling, which I truly love and feel like is a majorly important addition to my Bible journaling worship experience. I can also use the tip-in to "hide" a little bit of private journaling or prayer that I don't want to share on social media or with others at the current time. It's a very diverse, yet incredibly simple technique to add to your repertoire of art worship.

FINISHING TOUCHES:
A Repurposed Layered Tab Piece

TO FINISH OFF MY PAGE,
I wanted to add in some coordinating colors and textures from my layered tip-in piece for my tab collection at the top.

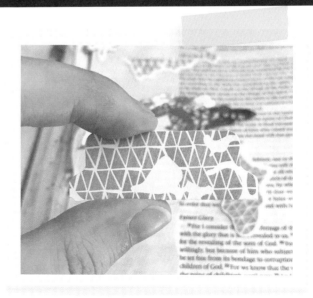

I pulled out my matching All People All Nations ephemera paper pieces and found two super pretty continent pieces. I set them aside along with the snipped-off portion of the gold foil doily and a small tabbie that perfectly encompassed the page theme.

In all honesty, this little tab collection took me a long time to play with to come up with something just right. I eventually pulled out my favorite tab paper punch and cut a standard tab piece from the large aqua-blue continent ephemera piece and continued to work the pieces again and again....

BUT STILL COULDN'T FIND THE PERFECT FIT!

TECHNIQUE · TECHNIQUE

Instead of getting frustrated or bothered and giving up, I took the extra time this tab piece was providing me and used it as an opportunity to dwell further on the passage and what God wanted to say to me during my devotion time on this page. Taking the time to be creative means our minds have the opportunity to zone out—or zone in, if you will—**to what God has to say to us.**

Sometimes it just takes
A LITTLE FINAGLING
and **A LITTLE LOVE**
and **A LITTLE CREATIVE**
re-purposing to get something just right.
AND I'M PRETTY SURE THAT'S EXACTLY THE LESSON GOD WANTED ME TO LEARN FROM ROMANS 8:28.

Can I get an amen, friends?

After a few more tries, I pulled out another paper punch and popped out a cute little banner piece from the pink continent ephemera and easily layered the rest of my tab piece together!

SUPPLIES · SUPPLIES

• Gold Doily
• Enamel Heart
• BandW Tabbie
• Glue Runner
• TAB Punch
• Tiny Attacher
• Fiskars 1" Banner Punch
• All People All Nations Ephemera

SECTION 2:7
CLINGING TO THE TRUTH

GALATIANS 5:1

Christ has set us free to live a free life. This truth is something I want to cling to. Sometimes we cage ourselves and allow the enemy's lies to shadow God's truth. So what better way to allow His truth to take root than to journal it out, right? Now, let's take flight and allow God to run rampart in our hearts.

A devotional book is another great way to journal and spend time in the Word. The beauty of this devotional book in particular is that not only does it have devotional content to inspire journaling ideas, but it also includes Scripture. As a beginner, another great bonus in journaling on this book is that all the pages already have some art, doodles, or elements in different color hues, helping you set the tone for your inspiration.

I will be journaling through day 75 of the devotional book-*100 days of Bible Promises*. This entry focuses on the truth of how Christ has set us free. As I read the devotional content it gives me the imagery of being caged, and how God lifts the door and says, "Fly, little one! Fly as God made you to!" Already my mind starts thinking of birds, flight, and feeling FREE. I already know that's the direction I want to go for my journaling.

SO OFF WE GO.

(EASY PEASY RIGHT?).

- **100 Days of Bible Promises by Shanna Noel**
- **Illustrated Faith Digital Set:**
  Print & Pray Shop This Little Nest by Kelly Bangs

I printed my digital content on a full-size sticker sheet and then cut out the different stickers for size and scale. Next, I laid them on the page to see which stickers would work in different areas of the page before making them permanent. The cute, colorful branch was one of my favorites, and though large in scale, the advantage of clear stickers is that we can cut them down if needed. Since I wanted it to look like it was coming off the edge of the page, I placed my sticker in between the already cute doodles under the number 75 so it would all blend in. The idea is to make it seem like everything is part of the page. The bird I chose to be perched on the prayer portion on the bottom right is large in scale; his tail feathers covered some of the wording. But this is an easy fix. All I did was cut the tail feathers and you don't even notice the difference; he is "perfectly perched."

I also wanted to include a birdhouse while still keeping in mind that I need to leave space for journaling. I decided to cut out the smaller floral birdhouse and use the post of one of the larger birdhouses. Again the versatility of clear stickers is that you can mix and match stickers seamlessly. I went ahead and placed the smaller scale birdhouse by first cutting the post to size and then placing the birdhouse over it.

NOW. LET'S WORK ON THOSE LITTLE NOOKS OF SPACE.

On the left page, there are small areas to incorporate smaller stickers.
I went ahead and cut out smaller birds,
the nest, and some feathers to tie them into the theme of the right page.

FOR FINISHING TOUCHES,

I added some wordfetti and a small flair with the word **"BE FREE."**

SUPPLIES · SUPPLIES

- Precision Scissors
- Adhesive Flair: Dear Lizzy
- Avery 15665 Clear Full Sheet Sticker Paper
- Illustrated Faith's Cardstock Sticker Booklet:
  Words "wordfetti"

FINISHING TOUCHES:
Stickers

SO NOW, WHAT DO WE DO WITH THE LEFTOVER STICKERS?

Let's do some tags
to use as picture prompts.

The bonus to this is they become re-usable if you want to later incorporate them in a Bible journaling page.

TECHNIQUE · TECHNIQUE

I started with two tags—one big and one small—and chose colors that matched the set. The larger one is mustard with a white design that mimics the roof of the birdhouse I chose. The smaller tag is hot pink with a pattern that mimics the embellishment I want to use. If you choose a tag with designs like I did, make sure it doesn't clash with your stickers. You can also use plain tags with a similar color scheme.

Let's start off with the larger tag. I wanted to break up the mustard print a bit, so I incorporated a larger light-blue doily and a smaller lilac doily. I folded them in half, layered them, and used the tape runner to attach them to the tag and each other. Next, I really wanted to use those bigger birdhouses that didn't get to use on the book, so since had already used the post on the book, I chose to use the birdhouses without them and layer them instead. Since the tag has a design, I placed my stickers on cardstock and cut them out

I wanted the larger birdhouse to be off-centered (right) and edging off the page.
I ran the tape runner towards the left side of the birdhouse and adhered it. For layering I chose a smaller birdhouse and adhered it with the tape runner. I cut out a small bird and the mountains (I only used three out of the cluster of five mountains) and attached it to cardstock and onto the tag. Last, I added some wordfetti, an embroidered flower sticker, and some matching sheer ribbon.

For the smaller tag, I added the birdhouse by attaching the sticker to cardstock and also placing it off-centered (left). I added a paper fan sticker and added one of the bird cut outs to the center. I finished it off with some puffy stickers and sheer ribbon.

- **Illustrated Faith Puffy Stickers: Prayer and Feather**
- **Embroidered Flower and Fan Sticker:**
  Maggie Holmes
- **A Large and Small Tag: Tim Holtz**
- **Illustrated Faith Stickers:**
  This Little Nest by Kelly Bangs
- **Ribbons: The Paper Studio**
- **110 lb. White Cardstock**
- **Dollies: Tim Holtz**

SUPPLIES SUPPLIES

PRACTICE HERE!

SECTION 3:1

GOD'S FAVOR IS FOR A LIFETIME

PSALM 30:4-5

LAQUISHA HALL

I admire how David reminds us to always thank God, even after experiencing His anger, which "is but for a moment." Just as parents are disappointed when their children mess up but don't hold on to their anger, so God loves us, no matter how many times we mess up. His favor is for a lifetime. **You might cry at night, but your joy (the favor of the Lord) is on its way!**

FIRST THINGS FIRST
Welcome to Watercolors

Bible watercoloring can be done on more than just watercolor paper—journaling Bibles are awesome. Many have been afraid to use the watercolor technique in a Bible because of how thin the pages are; however, watercolor is an excellent choice that can be used again and again after practicing and becoming comfortable.

FOR A SUCCESSFUL SESSION, GATHER THE FOLLOWING:

- Paintbrushes (variety of sizes)
- Cup of water
- Napkins
- Scrap paper
- Watercolor paints (cakes or liquid)
- A heat tool (optional)

Water brushes are like paint brushes but have a barrel of water attached to the end of them. Using water brushes will help you control the flow of water while you paint and help you squeeze the desired amount of water you want out of the brush onto your page. Traditional paint brushes are effective when the right amount of water and paint is applied.

Water is used for cleaning traditional paint brushes. If the water becomes too dark, freshen your cup. Otherwise, lighter or brighter colors can look muddy with continued use.

Napkins are used to blot your paint brush and oftentimes your page. Blotting your page with a napkin after watercoloring on it creates textured effects. For example, allow applied watercolor to dry a bit before blotting it.

Test the watercolor on scrap paper before applying it to the page. See if it is dark (heavily pigmented) or light (color heavily saturated with water) enough before using.

Side Tip: Heat tools dry the page as you work much faster than waiting. This can be a craft tool or a simple hair dryer.

TECHNIQUE · TECHNIQUE

With wet paintbrush bristles, immerse the tip of your brush in the color you would like to paint with. If you don't have the color you need, using the color wheel, mix colors to create it. Generously apply to the Bible page. The page may crinkle or curl as the water is applied, but it will flatten after drying.

Continue to apply the desired colors to the page. Don't worry about the page being wet, just don't allow it to become too wet—if you lift the page and can see the water seeping through on the opposite side you have applied too much water. Remember that the goal is to apply color using the watercolor effect.

Important: To prevent tearing and damage, do not attempt to do anything else to the page until it is completely dry.

- Pencil
- Paper Source Heat Tool
- Loew-Cornell Paintbrush
- Illustrated Faith Pen (.35)
- ESV Crossway Journaling Bible
- Faber-Castell PITT Artist Pen (B)
- Winsor & Newton Paintbrush and Watercolors

SUPPLIES · SUPPLIES

Adding your own, unique drawings to your Bible page can be so rewarding. Whether you are drawing a simple character or sketching designs or patterns, your custom illustrations will enhance the Scripture or verse that you desire to remember.

FOR A SUCCESSFUL SESSION, GATHER THE FOLLOWING:

- Traditional pencil
- Eraser
- Charcoal pencil for shading and detailing (optional)

If you watercolor your page first, you can erase pencil sketchings but be careful to not be heavy-handed— you could actually erase the water- color too! If you pencil sketch before watercoloring you will not be able to erase the pencil marks after the paint dries. Be sure you have drawn what you want to keep!

Pencil lightly to give yourself room for error and correction. After sketching your illustration, trace over the lines with ink, marker, or other bold writing device.

TECHNIQUE · TECHNIQUE

If you have a desire to draw on the page but do not consider yourself an artist, find an illustration online that you like. Print it in black and place it under your Bible page. You can trace the image from the page on your Bible. Remember to color in your illustration with a bold writing device when finished.

All images drawn do not have to be colored: they can simply be traced or shaded in to create a realistic look and feel to your art. Choosing an image to illustrate can be challenging. I often brainstorm what should be the focal point of the page, what I can successfully draw and what will be an image that when I see it again makes me think of the particular verse. For the first Bible page, I drew the image of a clock with the amount of time spent facing God's anger and the time we spend in His favor. When I see this page, the clock will remind me that my blessings will always outweigh whatever problems I face. On the second Bible page, I drew the image of a girl sitting under a tree. The tree, seemingly larger than life, represents God and the "shade" or safety that He provides in my life.

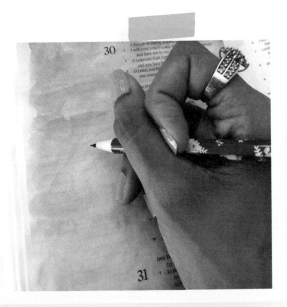

- **Pencil**
- **Eraser**
- **Illustrated Faith Pen**

HAND LETTERING IS SUCH A BEAUTIFUL ART FORM
that has been widely used in a variety of settings:

wedding invitations, greeting cards, framed art, and journaling Bibles!

The key to hand lettering is patience; the key to becoming better at hand lettering is to practice and remember that

PRACTICE MAKES PROGRESS (NOT PERFECTION)!

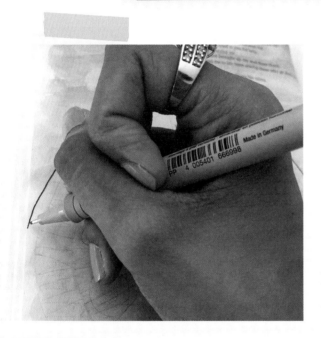

For a successful session, you will need a brush pen or a paint brush with watercolor or acrylic paint.

TECHNIQUE · TECHNIQUE

Side Tip: It is also great practice to create the letters with a pencil and then trace over them with pen. Finally, if you feel like you just cannot create the letters that you desire to, print them at the size you want the letters to be in your Bible, place them under the page you are working on, and trace them!

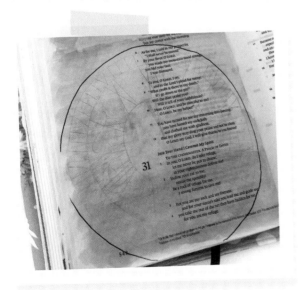

TECHNIQUE · TECHNIQUE

There are two strokes: upstrokes and downstrokes.

Upstrokes should be thin; downstrokes should be thick.

As you begin to write your letters, write slowly. Don't race to finish! Lettering is more of an art form than a writing habit—you want to create your letters and not just jot them down. Speed will come with practice. If you don't have a brush pen, you can draw the letters then make the places where a downstroke would be thicker.

Hand lettering in the margins key words that stuck out to you allows those words to pop! Also, hand lettering a page title gives the pages a focal point. On the first Bible page I created the word JOY using the clock to represent the letter *O*. I added "comes in the morning" to not only complete the Scripture but to remind me that my time is coming! For the second Bible page, I hand lettered "Cool Down" to remind me to rest in His shade when life becomes "too hot" or unbearable.

- Pencil
- Paper Source Heat Tool
- Loew-Cornell Paintbrush
- ESV Crossway Journaling Bible
- Faber-Castell PITT Artist Pen (B)
- Illustrated Faith Pen (.35), pencil
- Winsor & Newton Paintbrush and Watercolors

SUPPLIES · SUPPLIES

favor is for a lifetime

30

Joy Comes with the Morning

A PSALM OF DAVID. A SONG AT THE DEDICATION OF THE TEMPLE.

1 I will extol you, O LORD, for you have drawn me up
   and have not let my foes rejoice over me.
2 O LORD my God, I cried to you for help,
   and you have healed me.
3 O LORD, you have brought up my soul from Sheol;
   you restored me to life from among those who go down to the pit.

4 Sing praises to the LORD, O you his saints,
   and give thanks to his holy name.²
5 For his anger is but for a moment,
   and his favor is for a lifetime.³
   Weeping may tarry for the night,
   but joy comes with the morning.

6 As for me, I said in my prosperity,
   "I shall never be moved."
7 By your favor, O LORD,
   you made my mountain stand strong;
   you hid your face;
   I was dismayed.

8 To you, O LORD, I cry,
   and to the Lord I plead for mercy:
9 "What profit is there in my death,⁴
   if I go down to the pit?⁵
   Will the dust praise you?
   Will it tell of your faithfulness?
10 Hear, O LORD, and be merciful to me!
   O LORD, be my helper!"

11 You have turned for me my mourning into dancing;
   you have loosed my sackcloth
   and clothed me with gladness,
12 that my glory may sing your praise and not be silent.
   O LORD my God, I will give thanks to you forever!

comes in the morning

31

In You, O LORD, Do I Take Refuge

TO THE CHOIRMASTER. A PSALM OF DAVID.

1 In you, O LORD, do I take refuge;
   let me never be put to shame;
   in your righteousness deliver me!
2 Incline your ear to me;
   rescue me speedily!
   Be a rock of refuge for me,
   a strong fortress to save me!

3 For you are my rock and my fortress;
   and for your name's sake you lead me and guide me;
4 you take me out of the net they have hidden for me,
   for you are my refuge.

¹ Or to me, that I should not go down to the pit ² Hebrew to the memorial of his holiness (see Exodus 3:15) ³ Or and in his favor is life ⁴ Hebrew in my blood ⁵ Or to corruption

100 DAYS OF BIBLE PROMISES

Dive into God's unwavering truth, with topics such as freedom, comfort, grace, and gratitude. For 100 days, you'll find a featured Scripture, devotion and prayer, along with space for doodling, journaling, or writing notes.

ILLUSTRATING BIBLE

The Illustrating Bible has been specifically designed for the Bible journaler. Featuring thicker paper and margins twice the size of traditional journaling Bibles, this amazing Bible is spiral bound - lies flat - and square sized - great for social media sharing!

100 DAYS OF GRACE & GRATITUDE

Remember God's promises, goodness, and grace. For 100 days, you'll find a place for prayers, reflection, and creative expression, that will leave you gratefully reminded of just how loved you are.

ALL AVAILABLE AT
dayspring.com
AS WELL AS SEVERAL RETAIL STORES NEAR YOU.

MORE RESOURCES

Bible journaling has become a tremendously popular new way to connect with Scripture a creative way by combining faith and art. To learn more about Shanna Noel and the Bible journaling movement, vis **dayspring.com/biblejournaling** today

LIVE YOUR FAITH

Dear Friend,

This book was prayerfully crafted with you, the reader, in mind—every word, every sentence, every page—was thoughtfully written, designed, and packaged to encourage you...right where you are this very moment. At DaySpring, our vision is to see every person experience the life-changing message of God's love. So, as we worked through rough drafts, design changes, edits and details, we prayed for you to deeply experience His unfailing love, indescribable peace, and pure joy. It is our sincere hope that through these Truth-filled pages your heart will be blessed, knowing that God cares about you—your desires and disappointments, your challenges and dreams.

He knows. He cares. He loves you unconditionally.

BLESSINGS!
THE DAYSPRING BOOK TEAM

Additional copies of this book and
other DaySpring titles can be purchased
at fine bookstores everywhere.
Order online at dayspring.com
or
by phone at 1-877-751-4347